The Extra Mile

Celebrating
150 Years of Service
Government Agents in
British Columbia
1858-2008

The Extra Mile

Celebrating
150 Years of Service
Government Agents in
British Columbia
1858-2008

Service BC

Ministry of Labour and Citizens' Services

Fifth Draft: April 22, 2008

Copyright © 2008 B.C. Ministry of Labour and Citizens' Services

First Edition

Library and Archives Canada Cataloguing in Publication Data

Main entry under title:

The Extra Mile: Celebrating 150 years of Service Government Agents in British Columbia, 1858-2008. Available also on the Internet.

ISBN 978-0-7726-5951-4

1. Government information agencies - British Columbia - History. 2. Administrative agencies - Customer services - British Columbia - History. 3. Administrative agencies - British Columbia - History. I. Title: Celebrating one hundred and fifty years of service: Government agents in British Columbia, 1858-2008.

JL430.B74C44 2008   351.711   C2008-960058-4

Front-cover photo: Courtesy of Royal BC Museum, BC Archives

Cover designer: Rocket Science Design

Book design and layout: Calvin Jones, B.C. Public Affairs Bureau

Editor: Patricia Freeman

Stylus Editorial Associates

Printer: Queen's Printer

Printed in Canada

The Extra Mile

Celebrating
150 Years of Service:
Government Agents in
British Columbia
1858-2008

BRITISH
COLUMBIA
The Best Place on Earth

Table of Contents

Government Agent Service BC Centres in British Columbia Today

Atlin

Fort Nelson

Dease Lake

Stewart

Fort St. John

Chetwynd

Dawson Creek

Hazelton

Mackenzie

Smithers

Terrace

Houston

Fort St. James

Prince Rupert

Kitimat

Burns Lake

Prince George

Vanderhoof

Queen Charlotte

Quesnel

Valemount

Bella Coola

Williams Lake

100 Mile House

Golden

Clinton

Revelstoke

Kamloops

Salmon Arm

Invermere

Port Hardy

Lillooet

Ashcroft

Vernon

Nakusp

Campbell River

Powell River

Merritt

Kaslo

Sparwood

Courtenay

Squamish

Princeton

Penticton

Nelson

Fernie

Sechelt

Trail

Cranbrook

Port Alberni

Maple Ridge

Oliver

Grand Forks

Creston

Nanaimo

Chilliwack

Ucluelet

Ganges

Duncan

December 2004

Prepared by BC Stats

Lieutenant Governor

JUNE 19, 2008
GOVERNMENT AGENTS DAY

Her Majesty Queen Elizabeth II acknowledges Government Agents as "knowledgeable, service driven people respected for passion and commitment to their job" and proclaims June 19, 2008 as Government Agents Day.

Canaða
Province of British Columbia
A Proclamation

ELIZABETH THE SECOND, by the Grace of God, of the United Kingdom, Canada and Her other Realms and Territories, Queen, Head of the Commonwealth, Defender of the Faith

To all to whom these presents shall come — Greeting

WHEREAS Service BC's Government Agents are a unique, committed and valued part of communities across British Columbia, and

WHEREAS it is the vision of Service BC's Government Agents to provide easy access to government services, and

WHEREAS Service BC's Government Agents are knowledgeable, service driven people respected for passion and commitment to their job, and

WHEREAS British Columbians are asked to come together and celebrate 150 years of Government Agents and the provision of provincial government services, and

WHEREAS Our Lieutenant Governor, by and with the advice and consent of the Executive Council, has been pleased to enact Order in Council 903 on October 11, 2002;

NOW KNOW YE THAT We do by these presents proclaim and declare that June 19, 2008, shall be known as

"Government Agents Day"

in the Province of British Columbia.

IN TESTIMONY WHEREOF We have caused these Our Letters to be made Patent and the Great Seal of Our Province to be hereunto affixed.

WITNESS The Honourable Steven L. Point, Lieutenant Governor of Our Province of British Columbia, in Our City of Victoria, in Our Province, this eighth day of January, two thousand eight and in the fifty-sixth year of Our Reign.

BY COMMAND.

ATTORNEY GENERAL
AND MINISTER RESPONSIBLE FOR MULTICULTURALISM

✒ Foreword ✒

by Premier Gordon Campbell

*A*s we celebrate the sesquicentennial of the founding of the Colony of British Columbia and look back over the past 150 years, there is no question that the commitment of public servants is at the core of the remarkable growth, prosperity and transformation of our province.

Today's professional public service is a continuation of the legacy established by the first Government Agents a century and a half ago. Where the population of the entire fledgling colony in 1858 numbered little more than 30,000—most of them newly arrived gold miners—today's BC Public Service includes 30,000 dedicated individuals who every day work to preserve, protect and promote the unique social, cultural and economic diversity of British Columbia for the benefit of more than four million citizens.

It all began with the first handful of provincial representatives 150 years ago. As you'll read in this book, the lives and work of those early public servants was enormously challenging and often colourful. In countless ways, they shaped the early history of the colony and then the province of British Columbia, whether they were keeping the peace or recording weather data. The vast range of duties performed by early Government Agents in many ways reflects the great diversity of work carried out by the modern public service—then, as now, in even the most remote areas of our province. Even today, the Government Agents remain the primary point of contact between British Columbians and their government in communities large and small.

When you read the stories in this book, you'll learn not just about the history of Government Agents or the history of the public service, but about the vibrant history and spirit of British Columbia as a whole. Our history is something to celebrate and preserve because it is, in many ways, the history of a unique place filled with unique individuals that continue to influence who we are as a people and a province. The history of the public servants who have helped shape our province throughout the past 150 years is one in which we can all take pride.

On behalf of all British Columbians, I want to say thank you to the Government Agents past and present and to all the members of the BC Public Service who continue the legacy of building a stronger British Columbia.

GOVERNMENT AGENT TIMELINE
1858 — 2008

1858
The founding of the Crown Colony of British Columbia and the spreading word of gold discoveries. An estimated 20,000-50,000 people arrive in B.C.

Introduction

*A*T EVERY MOMENT OF EVERY YEAR IN EVERY DECADE for the past 150 years, employees of the British Columbia government have served the public. While they have done so under many job titles, the one thread that has continued unbroken to the present day is this: Government Agents exist to provide an extraordinary array of services.

The year before the Colony of British Columbia was formed, its first governor, Sir James Douglas, wrote a royal proclamation claiming for the colony all of the gold around the Fraser and Thompson rivers. On that day-December 28, 1857-only 300 settlers lived in Victoria. By the end of the next year, 2,500 more had moved in-and 30,000 miners were swarming the province looking for gold. Douglas needed officers to bring stability to the land, and so the first provincial representatives were born. Those officials were the first in a 15-decade-long line of employees who would carry out the will of government across British Columbia. The origins of every B.C. service provided in the province can be traced back to those roots.

The people who worked for the new Colony of British Columbia in 1858 and onwards performed the numerous tasks required of someone representing government in a frontier town. They enforced the law, kept the peace, legalized mining claims, performed marriage ceremonies, buried the dead, collected taxes, sold liquor licences, "took custody of lunatics" as one old document puts it, liaised with First Nations people, sheltered voters who had ridden vast distances to get into a village to cast their vote, recorded water tables, collected fees, levied fines, and inspected schools and hospitals. If there was anything else that needed doing on behalf of the capital, they did that too.

Known at first as magistrates or, because it was the time of the great Cariboo gold rush, gold commissioners, they set up office in their own homes, often as the sole provincial official in town. The term "Government Agent" first officially appeared in provincial yearbooks and legislative debates in 1873, although one photographic record circa 1865 uses it to describe Nicola's John Clapperton, and Governor Musgrave used the term in 1870. Within a few years, though, most Crown officers were called Government Agents.

In 1859, they served six districts: Hope, Yale, Lytton, Lillooet, Queensborough, and Douglas. By 1890, Government Agents' duties were set for the first time by order-in-council, and they were beginning to think of themselves as public servants. A year later, they worked in offices in 11 communities: New Westminster, East Kootenay, West Kootenay, Cariboo (Richfield), Cariboo (Quesnel), Cassiar, Yale, Kamloops, Okanagan, Nanaimo, and Clinton. During the 1970s and 1980s, Government Agents provided services to the public from access centres across the province, and today they work in 59 Service BC Centres, from Ganges on Saltspring Island to Atlin in the far north.

In 1977, the first attempt was made to write a job description of Government Agents-and found to be almost impossible. How could so many portfolios be contained within one definition? The attempt began with the statement, "The diversified duties of a Government Agent's position defy a concise Job Description." It went on to say, "Government Agencies are Service Organizations constantly changing in scope and jurisdiction, unlike one another, the major responsibilities being determined by the economic development of a given region. In the community a Government Agent is best known as a reliable source of knowledge on all governmental subjects and as an 'Ombudsman' when bureaucracy appears unfair."

The description included a long list of specific responsibilities to almost each B.C. ministry of the day. Under the Ministry of Finance, Government Agents were responsible for collecting provincial revenue and spending Crown funds on various projects. They also collected taxes and answered queries about them. Under the Provincial Secretary, Government Agents registered voters for elections and maintained the provincial voters list. They reported to the then Ministry of Energy, Transport and Communications regarding motor vehicle licences and recorded mineral claims for the Ministry of Mines. Twenty-four Government Agents worked in the late 1970s for the Ministry of the Environment as land commissioners and water recorders. For the Ministry of Health, they registered births, deaths, and marriages and, for the Ministry of Attorney General, administered the estates of everyone who died without a will and registered all bankruptcies. For the Ministry of Recreation and Travel, Government Agents issued no fewer than 39 separately classified hunting and fishing licences.

Government Agents also acted on behalf of landlords and assisted the public with grants and second mortgages for the Ministry of Consumer and Corporate Affairs. They issued electrical and gas permits and supervised the maintenance of public buildings for the B.C. Ministry of Public Works. Every single one of these tasks was to be conducted with "a high standard of service."

The job description concluded with the first mission statement ever written by any organization in provincial government history: "We are here to serve.... The

JUNE 1858
Governor James Douglas appoints revenue officers to collect taxes, administer proclamations and generally keep law and order. (This position is generally accepted as the first Government Agent, although they are not called that yet.)

public are not cold statistics, but flesh and blood persons with feelings and emotions like our own. The public are people who bring us their wants and it is our job to handle them as expeditiously and courteously as possible. Take care of the public. That's why we are here."

Government Agents have been liked, admired, respected, and revered for their services to communities throughout British Columbia for 150 years. They get to know their customers and sometimes befriend them. One customer service representative in 1991 said that when she went out for lunch in Maple Ridge, people called out to her cheerfully from across the street, "Hi, government lady." They knew who she was, and she knew them. Government Agents are to this day an integral part of the community. It is no wonder, then, that citizens' satisfaction rating of the Government Agents' branch, Service BC, is the highest of any regional public body in government.

SEPTEMBER 1858
Governor Douglas makes several appointments to the revenue officer position, which include land commissioner, water recorder, gold commissioner, and magistrate-setting a precedent for what is to come.

ᗌ Setting Up Shop ᗌ

*O*H, THOSE EARLY DAYS IN BRITISH COLUMBIA, when disputes were resolved with a fistful of knuckles and people could get a free lunch at Frank's bar in the capital city of Victoria. The first Government Agents saw it all.

PLANTING THE SEED

The Government Agency system was born in 1858 when the first governor of the new Colony of British Columbia, Sir James Douglas, appointed the first public servants to collect taxes and issue licences. On September 7, 1859, he created the new, unique office of gold commissioner with the Gold Fields Act. The title referred to officials who performed the duties laid out in mining legislation-although they also acted as governor, judge, justice of the peace, and conducted a host of other administrative and judicial duties. "Gold commissioner" was used until the more general title "Government Agent" came into use.

In July 1860, the first gold commissioner for the Cariboo was appointed to reside at Alexandria. By 1862, the events of the Cariboo gold rush had shown that Alexandria was the wrong location for this office, so it was closed.

From 1862 to 1865, the Cariboo was divided into two parts, Cariboo East with a gold commissioner at Quesnelle Forks, and Cariboo West with a gold commissioner at Williams Creek. In April 1865, Cariboo East and Cariboo West were united to form the District of Cariboo with the gold commissioner residing at Richfield. Barkerville soon became the actual administrative centre, but the official address remained Richfield until 1897.

The county court continued to sit at Richfield until 1914, when it moved to Quesnel. However, the office of the Cariboo gold commissioner remained at Barkerville until 1954, when all administrative functions were centralised at Quesnel.

A COUPLE OF FIRSTS

Because of their unique position as representatives of government in even the remotest regions of British Columbia, it fell to Government Agents-or magistrates and gold commissioners, as they were called in the province's colonial days-to take on whatever services needed to be done. Regardless of the assignments they were asked to do, they always did so to the best of their abilities.

In 1865, all Government Agents were asked to be hospital administrators, a task they said they perceived as thankless but nevertheless took on. They must have done a good job, because five years later the role was expanded to include hospital inspectors. This required monthly visits as well as occasional surprise visits to each hospital in their district to inspect patients' diets and hospitals' washing facilities.

St. Andrew's Hospital in Atlin, B.C.

It appears, though, that Government Agents embraced another task that fell to them 50 years later. Long before Environment Canada or nightly weather reports with high-tech maps and satellite imagery, who else should provide weather data but these tireless government workers? In the early 1900s, they acted as weathermen, painstakingly recording the state of the day's weather on behalf of the Province of British Columbia. Their service grew into a contract with the Dominion of Canada and then with the Meteorological Service of Canada.

Twice a day, from midnight to noon and from noon to midnight, Government Agent staff carefully recorded temperatures and the amount of precipitation and cloudiness, and made what today seem like curiously subjective remarks such as "cedar waxwings overhead" and "dandelion seed flying." Regardless, they were among the first to build a weather database.

1858-1929
Revenue collection, administration of justice, law and order, administration and disposal of natural resources, construction and maintenance of roads are the main functions of Government Agents.

Government Agents' detailed comments such as these in 1902 and 1908 became the model for Canada's official weather database.

A FREE LUNCH

Even back in the days when a bridge connected Government Street to James Bay, Victoria was a hospitable sort of place. Sidney Russell Almond, the Grand Forks Government Agent, described his first impressions during a visit to the young provincial capital in 1897. He drew a very different picture, of course, from the city today—and of one enterprising restaurateur:

> "Victoria was only a small place when I first saw it. There was nothing south of the bridge on Government street, only the buildings and a few nice private houses. I can remember thinking that the legislative buildings were a curious lot of structures, and they struck me as being as ill-fitted for office purposes inside as they were odd and toy-like outside. The bridge over the bay to them was a rickety cart of [an] affair and not a very pretentious approach to them. The mud-flats which they called a bay stank like everything, especially when the tide was out. In the other

direction there was not much beyond Johnston street, and not much out along Fort street or Yates street.

"One place that the lawyers and doctors and everyone frequented was Frank's, on the right hand and down Yates street, I think it was. A fine free lunch he has and a fine crowd he had in to partake of it!! But they were not laggards in buying liquid refreshment to wash the free lunch down. From the number of bars in Victoria in those times, and the crowded patronage in them, you would say that the principal occupations of Victorian businessmen and professional men was drinking.

"At the corner of Yates and Government streets was Campbell the tobacconist. His place was a great resort also where you could hear the local and political news of the day, and where on a board you would find a copy of telegraph dispatches to the newspapers giving a few items of world news."

Fort Street, Victoria, in the 1800s.

PEACE, ORDER, AND GOOD GOVERNMENT

Despite the occasional murder and robbery, crime rates were low in British Columbia's early years. This was due, in large part, to the hardy men who acted as magistrates, gold commissioners, revenue collectors, land commissioners, Indian agents, and coroners-in other words, the Government Agents. They were expected to make up the rules as they went along and to use their moral authority against a backdrop of guns and knives frequently being pointed in their direction.

In his papers, Judge Matthew Baillie Begbie showed that he understood that not

1858-1990s
Government Agents act as marriage commissioners-and still can upon special dispensation.

1864
First magistrate office in New Westminster, at the time the capital of the Colony of British Columbia.

he but this band of men kept the colony's reputation for peace, order, and good government:

> "The criminal statistics of the colony appear highly favourable when placed beside those of any other gold-producing country. Crimes of violence are extremely rare; highway robberies almost unknown... Stabbing and pistoling, so common in the adjacent territories, are almost unheard of on the British side of the line; although the population is composed of the same ingredients. I should be sorry to have it supposed that I am vain enough to attribute most fortunate state of things purely to myself. I know that what is due to the Executive, in all its branches, particularly to the excellent and invaluable magistrates, who, scattered at great intervals, generally with only two or three constables apiece, enforce observance of the laws almost entirely by their moral influence."

These pioneering men laid the foundation for generations of Government Agents to come.

CROWDED HOUSE

For many years, housing was provided to Government Agents, a practice that continued right into the 1980s in more isolated communities. Sometimes it was a necessary perk to get someone to move to a particular location.

However, the quality of the accommodation varied from community to community, and often staff had to make do with rustic and difficult conditions until improvements could be made. The number of letters on the subject sent to Victoria show that it has not always been easy to be a Government Agent in the province's rough-and-tumble regions.

In one recorded instance in the 1920s, a gold commissioner appealed to government for improvements to his living quarters, which he had to share with 30 high school students.

By October 1927, the issue was somewhat alleviated when he received new lodgings and, eventually, a furnace to go with them. However, with the Depression, matters got progressively worse until 1939, when the MLA got involved in the matter-but by then the home was not worth the price of repairs.

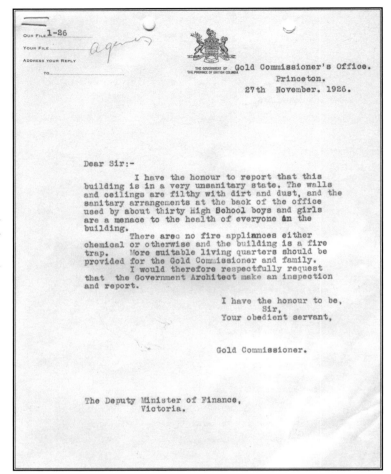

Princeton's gold commissioner writes to the Deputy Minister of Finance in November 1926, asking for help with his crowded living quarters.

BEGGING FOR A RAISE

Not only did Government Agents have to struggle with difficult living quarters, but tales abound from the 1880s right up until at least 1945, of requests for pay raises or cost of living bonuses because they could not make ends meet.

No set salary existed, and increases were granted haphazardly; what one minister granted, another denied. As well, each Government Agent was expected to pay for certain things, such as boarding voters in their homes, while at the same time draw part of their salary from the fines and fees they levied. After these expenses were subtracted, little or no money was left for their pay. It appears that if one raised the issue,

1865
Marriage ordinance is introduced. Government Agents are appointed to perform civil marriages and issue marriage certificates. They take on the role of hospital administrators. This continues into the late 1960s.

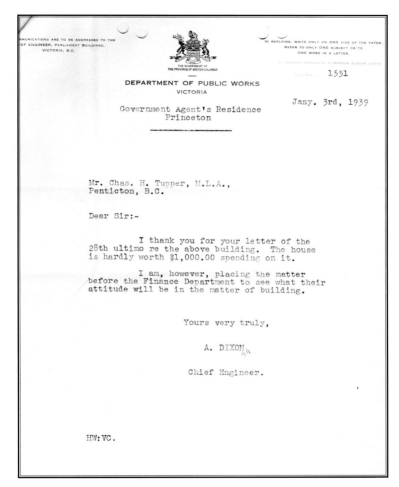

In 1939, the gold commissioner is finally told his house is not worth fixing.

an amount was negotiated and that was the end of it; the Government Agent the next valley over could be making more or less in remuneration for the same duties.

One Government Agent who acted as returning officer in a late 1880s election, for example, complained about the mere $10 he was offered for the task. He "declined the acceptance of so small a sum, upon the ground (to say nothing of the trouble & inconvenience as the Poll is held at my house) that for some 2 or 3 days I have to board and lodge the voters, and their horses, at my own expense." The same officer, in another letter to the colonial government, requested a salary of $150 per month, including board and his own horse.

Stephen Hoskins, the Government Agent for Smithers, wrote on May 9, 1923, "It is more than 10 years ago that I was sent to this district as Government [Agent], and during that time I appear to have received only $7.66 per month increase."

And on May 12, 1923, Thomas Herne, Government Agent for Prince Rupert, wrote,

> "I notice… that I am to receive a salary of $175.00, the same as I received in South Fort George. Now Mr. McMullin was receiving $195.00 in this Agency, and I consider that I should be entitled to receive the same

Gold Commissioner C. Nichols writes again to Victoria in 1942, this time to ask for a cost of living bonus.

```
Box 19.

                                          Princeton, B. C.,
                                          May 6th, 1942.


Mr. Norman Baker,
Civil Service Commissioner,
Parliament Buildings,
VICTORIA, B. C.

              RE: Cost of Living Bonus

Dear Sir:

          As I understand the cost of living bonus is supposed
to compensate for the increased cost of living I think that
cases like mine should be considered, even though the value of
the perquisites plus the salary comes to over $2100.00.

          My salary is $150.00 per month, the perquisites
considered on the house valued for superannuation and taxation
purposes at $33.50, making a total of $183.50. However after
deductions, the cheque that I receive each month amounts to
$132.98. I have kept track of my expenditures for the last
twelve months and the average are as follows:

          Groceries, milk, etc.          62.00
          Meat                           17.00
          Insurance - Including int. on
                            loan         15.00
          Doctor & Dentist               5.00
          School books & Supplies        5.00
          Music lessons for children     8.00
                                        $112.00

          This leaves a balance of $20.98 to pay for other
expenditures including holidays which I have been unable to
afford for the family for several years. In addition to this
I am also expected to contribute to everything of a charitable
or patriotic nature and also to do a certain amount of enter-
taining.
```

1867
Some Government Agents are appointed as justices of the peace.

1869
Government Agents are appointed as deputy collectors of customs, collectors of road ordinance (tax), and postmasters.

salary he was getting as I am taking over all his duties that he performed here. I am an old Civil Servant, and consider that if I am good enough to fill the offices of Mr. McMullin, I think that I should receive the salary that he was getting."

The solution in Prince George was to make the Government Agent a magistrate whereby the city, not the province, was obligated to pay the additional funds.

Show Us the Money

Government Agents often felt underpaid, yet they managed millions of dollars at a time on behalf of government. In those days of hands-on cash and no credit cards and online payment, they had to physically store and then transfer all that gold bullion and cash down to the capital.

After the officers had paid all the costs of running local operations-from paying salaries to their own travel costs for inspecting hospitals, schools, and mineral claims-out of the revenue they had collected, they were responsible for getting the balance to Treasury in Victoria. But the lag of timing in the delivery more often than not left Treasury short on funds. Notes from the colonial and then the provincial Treasury

The colonial secretary advises a Government Agent to advance the accumulated "large balance" of $6,752 to Victoria.

reminded Government Agents to forward funds to the capital city on a regular basis so that it had sufficient funds to run government.

Tempting as it might have been, they never hid the funds. Officials regularly sent statements to Victoria of exactly how many pounds they had on hand for the business of government. And then they delivered the funds there-eventually.

To Recycle or Not to Recycle

In the heady days between the beginning of the 20th century and the outbreak of World War I, progress seemed inevitable and all things seemed possible. If a community had reached the stage of development in which a courthouse was deemed necessary by the government, this was proof that the community's renown had reached the corridors of power in far-off Victoria. Such a facility might have been important as an administrative and judicial centre and boosted the local economy, but the symbol rather than the substance galvanized townsfolks' ambitions.

In 1903, the new Greenwood courthouse opened, and Government Agent William McMynn was deeply involved with the project. The task of furnishing the building fell to him and, in the spirit of Government Agents' tradition of keeping costs down, he chose to purchase furniture from a hotel that had gone bankrupt.

The editor of the Boundary Creek Times was so incensed by this that he took the unfortunate Government Agent to task:

> "No man putteth new wine in old bottles, but in furnishing the Courthouse the Government Agent has scorned this old maxim. The major portion of the furnishings that adorn the new building have done duty for years in one of the principal hotels of Greenwood, & not being considered worth moving to another locality were turned over to the B.C. Government for use in the new Courthouse.
>
> "They may have been purchased at a bargain. It may be true business. It may be true economy in public service, but in our opinion, the province is yet well able to properly furnish its public institutions without indulging in...(sic) secondhand business."

The editor might have reacted differently if McMynn had purchased brand new furnishings for the courthouse; he might have chosen to castigate him for his profligate squandering of taxpayers' money!

1871
Government Agents are appointed as registrars of voters, registrars of vital statistics/births, deaths and marriages, court registrars (County and Supreme Courts), stipendiary magistrates, and returning officers for elections.

Frugally furnished: the
Greenwood courthouse and
police headquarters.

1871/72–1880s
Government Agents perform the function of constable/sheriff and goaler; this role is removed from the Government Agent in favour of forming a separate police department with its own commissioner.

⚒ Toughing it Out in the Early Days ⚒

*F*ROM "CAPTURING LUNATICS" TO SETTLING SKIRMISHES over mining disputes, early Government Agents had to put up with a great deal. As representatives of the newly formed Colony of British Columbia and often the sole government official in an isolated community, they were frequently called upon to settle arguments and uphold the law.

PUBLIC ACCOUNTS EQUALS PUBLIC HISTORY

A great deal can be learned about the history of Government Agents by researching the Public Accounts, which are available from 1871 to the present day.

For his work in 1872 as Omineca's gold commissioner, for example, W.H. Fitzgerald received $3,073.32. (Gold commissioners' salaries were among the highest in government at this time.)

A page from the 1872 Public Accounts details pay received for interesting services rendered:

G. Hadican	Keep of Horses	$15
M. Hayden	Hay for Horses	$240
Rev. D. Holmes	Firewood for Gaol	$24.50
W. Mares	Digging Graves	$12
W. & J. Wilson	Clothing for Prisoners	$270
S.W. Herring	Milk for Sick Prisoners	$2.81
A. Thomas	Capturing escaped Lunatic	$10
E.A. Sharpe	Capturing escaped Lunatic	$9.25
S. Thomas	Boarding an idiotic man	$24.

A MURDEROUS FIRST

The horrible murder on December 8, 1879 of Constable John Tennant Ussher of Kamloops made him, it is believed, the first Government Agent in British Columbia to die in the line of duty.

It began with a horse theft and the infamous McLean gang, "the most worthless set of Vagabonds that ever lived in any country," as one contemporary described them. The four thugs-brothers Allan McLean, 25; Charlie McLean, 17; and Archie McLean, 15; along with Alex Hare, 17-were well known to most of the town's law-abiding citizens for their brutal ways.

Before arresting the McLean gang for stealing a horse, Ussher swore in two special constables and rallied a local rancher named McLeod. The posse set out on the gang's trail. Ussher knew the boys and, although he had been warned that he was making a mistake not to take more men with him, presumed they would not resist. He and his constables left their revolvers behind-a fatal mistake.

As Ussher and his men approached the McLean camp on horseback, the gang lay waiting in ambush. Suddenly shots rang out, Ussher's horse was startled, and he fell off. Hare jumped from behind a tree and approached the defenceless Ussher, who begged them not to kill him saying he had not come to harm them. But Hare heard none of it and stabbed him several times in the neck. Then the youngest of the McLean brothers, Archie, shot him in the face and killed him. The rest of the posse fought furiously, and rancher McLeod was wounded in the face before they retreated and rode back to Kamloops for help. In the meantime, the McLeans stole Ussher's coat, boots, gloves, handcuffs, and horse.

The gang fled and terrorized several other neighbouring families and, for target practice, shot and killed shepherd John Kelly as he sat watching his flock. Eventually a second posse tracked them down to an old cabin where a standoff and shootout ensued for several days before the gang members finally surrendered.

Their first trial, conviction, and hanging sentence, on March 13, 1880 in New Westminster, was overturned on a technicality, and while awaiting a new trial the criminals made several unsuccessful escape attempts. They were retried, convicted and again sentenced to hang. Finally, on January 31, 1881, all four were hanged in New Westminster.

PROTECTING FIRST NATIONS' RIGHTS

As early as the spring of 1855, Governor James Douglas, through his magistrates, made great efforts to uphold First Nations' rights and to treat them fairly. Yet he was troubled by what he saw and wrote letters to the colonial secretary about what he suspected was the "mismanagement" of natives by American authorities.

Three years later, Douglas was still trying to instil fair treatment toward native

1872

Government Agents are appointed as coroners and notaries public. They continue to be coroners into the 1990s. Some agents still hold the title of notary public.

peoples. After meeting with a group of mainly American miners, he wrote that they "were permitted to remain merely on sufferance; that no abuses would be tolerated; and that the laws would protect the rights of the Indian, no less than those of the white man."

This effort came to life in the Harold Hockings affair. Local miner Hockings used the services of a Sto:lo guide, Charlie Joe, to take him up river. When Joe asked for payment, Hockings told him instead to leave the area or he would sink Joe's canoe and shoot him.

The oral history passed down through tribal elders says that Joe felt his only recourse was to come back up river and kill the man at a time of his choosing. Then he remembered a conversation he had had with Chartres Brew that the Queen's men would protect the rights of an Indian man as much as a white man.

Joe eventually related his story to Brew, who was tasked with keeping the peace between natives and the many thousands of miners scattered along the Fraser River. He referred to Hockings as another x-welitems, which translates roughly into "hungry people" or "greedy people."

Some days later, Brew bumped into a man on a sandbar and asked him to produce his miner's licence. The man handed it over and was promptly told, "Harold Hockings, unless you immediately pay the $20 you owe Charlie Joe for your canoe trip, you are under arrest."

Hockings paid. He was efficiently issued a receipt for the $20 plus court fees, and Joe was given what was owed him.

Beaver Lake

Government Agents made other efforts to keep First Nations' rights from being violated.

A resident of Beaver Lake, B.C., and the Cariboo's first gold commissioner, Philip Henry Nind, responded unhappily to any unfair treatment of First Nations. He filed a complaint with his jurisdiction on January 4, 1861:

> "I address you as one of the residents at Beaver Lake and beg that you will let the purport of this letter be known as widely as possible. Information was brought to me yesterday that several outrages have lately been committed on Indian men and women who are residing at Beaver Lake during the winter; the complainants stated that women

had been dragged off against their will, violence employed towards them and their husbands, fathers or other relations when attempting to defend them, beaten and otherwise ill used, the treatment they were subjected to leading to the supposition that Indians are regarded as no better than beasts of burthen [sic] or convenience for worse purposes.

"I wish to intimate to all persons who frequent your house and the locality of Beaver Lake that such is not the case in the eyes of the law, and that the British Government always had afforded protection to the meanest of its subjects and will continue to do so without distinction of race or colour. If an Indian comes to me with a complaint against a white man I am just as much bound to receive that complaint and institute proceedings against the offender as if the complaint were brought by one white man against another, it being one of the first principles of English law, (by which this colony is governed), that before the law all men are equal and entitled to equal privileges and rights, such is the plain sale laid down and I am determined to uphold it without fear or favour."

Colonial records indicate that Nind did not have to write a second letter and that an "attitude adjustment" did occur at Beaver Lake. Court records of the period are not complete, and it is not known if any band members came forward to press charges.

Clinton: The Belle of the Ball

In the midst of the hustle and bustle of a quickly growing province, in 1862 The Junction was a hub of activity, because two roads connected it to Yale, Lillooet, Lytton, Barkerville, and Wells, busy places during the Cariboo gold rush. It still is. However, the town goes by a different name now. It was eventually renamed 47 Mile House and then rechristened Clinton in June 1963, after the British Duke, Henry Tiennes Pelham Clinton.

Clinton's first Government Agent was Charles Pope, appointed in May 1872. As such officers frequently did, he held many posts: clerk of the bench, constable, clerk of the Clinton polling division, toll collector, and postmaster. Notably, Pope died in the asylum at New Westminster in 1878.

The original government buildings in The Junction were constructed on the west side of Cariboo Road, across the highway from the present provincial buildings. Then in 1926, a new building was built but burned down before it could be occupied. Rebuilt on the same footprint a year later, it housed the Government Agent, courts,

1873
Government Agents are appointed as registrars of titles and bills of sale; recorders of cattle brands; collectors and assessors of land tax, Court of Appeal for Road Tax; and sheriffs.

The term "Government Agent" first officially appears in provincial yearbooks and legislative debates.

police, and the jail. An RCMP officer and his family lived on the second floor of the building-the staff coffee room and the main floor washroom still have bars on the windows from the rooms' old days as jail cells.

Fourteen more Government Agents followed Pope until, in 1997, the Clinton Government Agent position was merged with other communities with which the town had a close connection, and Clinton became co-managed from Kamloops and, later, from Lillooet.

Clinton's local dignitaries.

Today the thriving little community boasts the oldest annual celebration in Canada: the Clinton Annual Ball, a formal gala for which, in the 1800s, women ordered gowns from Paris and men wore their best "bib and tucker." The first ball was held in January 1868 at the Clinton Hotel and lasted a week. As its reputation grew over the years, people came from as far away as Barkerville and even San Francisco. The ball continues to this day, with the 141st annual ball in May 2008, except that tickets cost $50 instead of $5. Of course, Government Agents had a hand in that too; until the 1970s, those desiring to attend the ball had only to ask, and their Government Agent made all the arrangements.

THE POLICE INSPECTOR'S GRUESOME TALE

Early in the last century, until the railway came in 1930, Pouce Coupe was the main centre for the Peace River Block south of the Peace River. With the railway's decision to build to Dawson Creek, the centre moved gradually to the new town, but the government offices remained in Pouce. The Government Agent, public works superintendent, provincial police inspector, provincial assessor, sheriff's office, social welfare, and provincial correspondence school all maintained offices in the courthouse.

From 1917 to 1920, Constable G.J. Duncan worked in Pouce Coupe doing many of the things a Government Sub-Agent would have done at the time; he registered births, deaths, and marriages, and acted as official administrator, mining recorder, and game warden.

Pouce Coupe's Provincial Police Constable G.J. Duncan.

After a gap of 29 years elsewhere, Duncan returned to Pouce Coupe in 1949 as police inspector, only to hear an amusing story about his predecessor, Constable Anderson. A murder had been committed, and Anderson was called upon to produce evidence before the nearest B.C. police doctor, who happened to be in Kamloops, hundreds of miles away. This was a real problem when the only means of travel was by water and dog team. So he solved the difficulty by cutting off the victim's head where the injury was located. Arriving in the doctor's office, Anderson put the gruesome relic on the table and said, "doctor, what did this man die of?" The doctor looked up in horror and amazement, and said, "Why, decapitation of course."

The "Grouse Creek War"

Whenever the burly men who made their living as miners argued over their claims, it was up to the gold commissioners to resolve the problem. Many disputes were settled peacefully, sometimes through on-the-spot negotiation, sometimes through a more formal process called a "miner's court." Sometimes they could not be resolved and led

1874-75
The term "Government Agent" is defined under the Interpretation Act.

1875
Government Agents are appointed as cemetery trustees.

to out-and-out battles like the so-called Grouse Creek War of 1877-78.

It all started when two gold commissioners accidentally granted the same title to two different mining companies. In 1864, Cariboo East Gold Commissioner Peter O'Reilly granted the Grouse Creek Bedrock Flume Company of Victoria the rights to some land at Grouse Creek, near Barkerville, for 10 years. The following year O'Reilly was transferred to the Kootenays, the Cariboo East and Cariboo West districts were amalgamated, and W.G. Cox became the Cariboo's new gold commissioner.

The Grouse Creek Bedrock Flume Creek Company ran out of money in 1866 and appeared to abandon the site. The local Canadian Company applied for rights to it, and New Westminster's gold commissioner, Warner Spalding, granted mineral title.

However, several months later the Grouse Creek Bedrock Flume Company re-negotiated for its rights to the claim and was reinstated. The Canadian Company, of course, objected, and the case returned to miners' court under Spalding who, not unsurprisingly, found for the Grouse Creek Bedrock Flume Company and ordered the Canadian Company miners to withdraw. They refused.

In 1867, an injunction was issued to enforce the order against the Canadian Company to abandon the claim, but its miners ignored it, and tempers flared. A warrant was issued for their arrest for such disobedience. The miners forcefully resisted an

Colonial officials at rest circa 1870. Judge Matthew Baillie Begbie, hatless, at left with dog; Governor Frederick Seymour sitting on hay bail in centre; Chief Commissioner of Lands and Works Joseph W. Trutch laying at centre with dog and gun; and chief sheriff and former gold commissioner of Lillooet, Andrew C. Elliott, sitting beside Trutch.

attempt to execute it. Prepared for battle, the local gold commissioner swore in 20 to 30 special constables to oust them from the grounds and arrest them, but the miners gathered 500 supporters and prepared to meet force with force. The commissioner reported the situation to Governor Seymour, who came to Barkerville with Judge Begbie, Colonial Secretary Arthur N. Birch, and Chief Commissioner of Lands and Works, Joseph W. Trutch.

Seymour persuaded the Canadian Company to leave the area with the promise of a new trial. A few of the company were arrested but spent an agreeable time in jail, where their sympathizers supplied them with bountiful grog.

On September 4, 1867, Chartres Brew, an experienced magistrate and the chief of police in New Westminster, was appointed gold commissioner and ordered to take temporary charge of the District of Cariboo. He accompanied Chief Justice Joseph Needham, Vancouver Island's chief justice, to Richfield courthouse near Barkerville, for the investigation of the dispute. Needham decided in favour of the Grouse Creek Company. The Canadian Company finally accepted this, thereby peacefully ending the "Grouse Creek War."

WILLIAM COX AND THE GREAT RACE

Methods of resolving mining disputes have evolved over British Columbia's 150 years; today's Government Agents rely on computers to acquire mineral tenure by electronic map selection. But in the early days, Government Agents had to be far more innovative, as the following example from the Cariboo gold rush illustrates.

William G. Cox had taken over from Peter O'Reilly as gold commissioner at Richfield in March 1863, when O'Reilly left the Cariboo to take up his duties as chief gold commissioner.

One day two miners got into a bitter dispute over the ownership of a claim and brought the matter before Cox for settlement. He heard them out and then solemnly decided that of a given day the two claimants should come to the courthouse and, when Cox gave the signal, run to the disputed ground. The first one there would get the ground! Now, that is one way to settle an argument.

1876
Andrew Charles Elliott, a former Government Agent in Lillooet, becomes British Columbia's fourth premier.
Government Agents are appointed as collectors of school tax.

Riding Through the Gold Rush

*E*VERYONE KNOWS ABOUT THE CALIFORNIA GOLD RUSH, but in the late 1800s, British Columbia's resources elicited every bit the same hysteria. Desperados and refined gentlemen came from all over Canada and the United Kingdom to try their chances at making it big in the province's gold fields.

GOLD FEVER

Lured by the smell of gold, Thomas Elwyn left Ireland for British Columbia hoping to strike it rich. However, he spent only a few years in the mines and many more in service to the new Colony of British Columbia, formed in 1858, the same year he arrived. Little did he know that he would become a major authority figure during the Cariboo gold rush.

Governor Douglas, who was deeply in need of men who could keep law and order in the gold fields, convinced Elwyn to take a government job instead of becoming a miner. Described as "a shrewd, clear-headed man," with considerable executive ability and an untarnished record for "probity, sincerity and manliness," Elwyn was perfect for the job.

Ironically, his roles as chief of police in Yale, assistant gold commissioner, and magistrate in Lillooet, and commander of several gold escorts from the Cariboo mines took him right to the heart of the gold rush. In 1862, he was made the second gold commissioner for the Cariboo after Commissioner Nind left following a nervous breakdown caused by working

Miner and Gold Commissioner Thomas Elwyn.

20-hour days trying to keep up with the paperwork generated by all the miners making and selling claims.

Elwyn eventually resigned due to a conflict of interest and followed his passion for prospecting. He owned a share in a gold claim on Williams Creek that had "become so valuable," he said, "that I cannot in justice to myself abandon it." Miners petitioned to keep the hugely popular Elwyn on anyway, because he had earned their trust by dealing fairly with them, but to no avail.

Although for the next few years he was officially a miner, he must have missed his old job; he occasionally helped government with such things as expeditions to Bute Inlet to arrest murderers, to Quesnel to extend a telegraph line, and to the Stikine River to help a mining party explore the area.

In 1871, Elwyn drove a band of cattle from Barkerville to Tête Jaune Cache, B.C., as winter provisions for a Canadian Pacific Railway survey party. Subsequently he is said to have been "engaged in the [Hudson's Bay Company]'s service on the steamer Otter and other vessels." Finally, on November 7, 1877, he was appointed to his last position as deputy provincial secretary, which he held until his death.

Contrary to his youthful dreams of fortune, Elwyn had had to borrow money from friends and relations "to carry him through." When all of his debts were paid, his estate amounted to less than $100.

How to Gain Friends and Win Elections

A minor squabble about the location of town officials' offices erupted in Lillooet in the late 1800s. It is an indication of how much gold was passing through town in those days.

On July 7, 1899, The Prospector published an article saying that the office of gold commissioner should be in Lillooet rather than inconvenient Clinton. It recommended the town's Government Agent, C. Phair, as a man capable of handling the position and went on to state threateningly that "the government should make the change as soon as possible and gain friends in this portion of the province."

Action on the matter was initially rather slow, although eventually expedited by the 61 per cent drop in the popular vote in the 1900 general election. Government finally reacted, and in 1903, The Prospector announced that Lillooet Mining Division was to have its very own gold commissioner, Phair.

Evidently the administration also regained its friends, because the local Conservative candidate was acclaimed into a majority government in 1903.

1877
Government Agents are appointed as inspectors of mines.

Second Only to Wells Fargo

For a long period during the mid-20th century Ashcroft's Government Agent was housed in Ashcroft's historical British Columbia Express (BCX) building.

The BCX, a stagecoach passenger and parcel delivery service, arrived in Ashcroft in 1886. With 100 bright red and yellow six-passenger stagecoaches pulled by six-horse teams, the BCX was second only to Wells Fargo in the United States for the size and scope of its operation. It carried supplies more than 1,000 miles to the gold fields and settlers in the Fraser Canyon, the Nicola Valley, the Okanagan, Lillooet, and Fort George. At its peak, the BCX was the town's biggest employer, with an office, freight and wagon warehouses, livery stables, houses for employees, barns, corrals, and fields for the horses on the outskirts of town.

The original office building was replaced in 1912, but with the increase of improved roads and automobile traffic and the decline of the Cariboo as a mining centre, the BCX survived for only another three years. The Ashcroft Cannery purchased the solid new building for its head office. Then, in 1925, the provincial government bought it as the new courthouse and government office facilities.

Government Agent Bill Munro worked here from 1954 to 1957. He normally worked alone in the big, drafty building, which was usually too cold in the winter and too hot in the summer. Every year, when it was time to renew motor vehicle licences, Bill Ketchum, Ashcroft's telegraph operator, was hired to help with the rush of people who left paying their $1.00 annual licence fee to the last minute. Munro also had company when the circuit judge from Williams Lake held court in the building each month.

The big back room had a raised dais and a look of formality. Munro, working out front, was kept busy swearing in witnesses. On a daily basis, he kept track of the town's births, marriages, and deaths in his big ledgers, sold hunting and fishing licences, kept mining records and acted as clerk of the peace. He locked up the records each night in the massive walk-in safe in the centre of the building.

The BCX building, now a private residence lovingly preserved by its current owners, continues to be an important part of the community. The massive vault that once held the gold and other valuables en route via stage coach is now their (very secure) bathroom!

The Start of the Wild Horse Creek Gold Rush

The first Government Agent office in the Kootenays was in the famous old placer mining camp, Wild Horse Creek. The pioneer town was built by the many prospectors that came to the area. Eventually the agency office moved for awhile to a place called

Galbraith's Ferry, now known as Fort Steele, and then again in 1904 to Cranbrook.

Coincidentally, in the 1800s, a Robert Galbraith owned and operated a boat named Galbraith's Ferry that transported mostly miners down the Kootenay River. The same Galbraith also served in the provincial legislature and in later years was appointed Indian agent.

In Cranbrook in the 1930s, J.E. Kennedy, a mining recorder in the Government Agent office there, received a request for information that would lead him on a historical search. While he was compiling material to respond to the request, Kennedy came across a letter written on August 1, 1865 and an interesting piece of history.

A prospector named Joseph Ashley had written the letter, signing his name with an X. Six others had signed it as well, attesting that he was their guide at the digs and justifying his claim. In his letter, Ashley was claiming the reward for his discovery of gold at Wild Horse Creek.

In the autumn of 1863, his letter said, he had been prospecting in the vicinity and found gold "in paying quantities." A Mr. Linklighter from the Hudson's Bay Company had paid him $150 in gold dust, but now Ashley sought the full reward. He had struck it rich. This drew attention from far afield to the locality and its gold, and it was not long before the big rush started for Wild Horse Creek.

No one will likely ever know whether Ashley was actually paid the reward. The oldest mining records in the Cranbrook government office only go back to 1891 because everything in the first office was destroyed; miners had set fire to the building to get at the rich ground underneath, leaving nothing but a pile of ashes.

IN SEARCH OF GOLD

In 1898, 48-year-old James Fraser had been running a profitable mining company in Vancouver, where he lived with his wife and five young sons. The city's enormous growth earlier in the century had turned to depression by then, and the Klondike gold rush was sparking everyone's imagination, including Fraser's-especially when his business partner ran off to the United States with the company funds. So Fraser, his accountant, his office boy, and two surveyor friends left home in search of Yukon gold. They took two horses, 11 dogs, and enough supplies for a year.

Their first stop was Nanaimo harbour, on February 8, 1898, in the cold and rain, with the dogs and horses lashed to the front decks of a steamer. Two of the dogs died when some crates fell on the deck. Six days later Fraser's party arrived in chaotic and lawless Skagway, Alaska and then rode up the White Pass, watched all the while by

1878
The first mention of Government Agents appointed to administer the Chinese Tax Act.

Mounties, who were ensuring that everyone who continued had at least a ton of supplies. Carrying this much, each stage of the route meant gruelling multiple trips back and forth hauling supplies.

Fraser and his party finally reached the great tent city at Lake Bennett in March. Rather than wait for the ice to melt, the intrepid group headed through the ice blocks on top of the lakes until they reached the Yukon River, where they constructed a raft. Half of their supplies fell overboard, but they reached Fort Selkirk at the intersection of the Yukon and Pelly rivers. Knowledgeable about the mining business, Fraser's crew knew they would be a year too late for the Klondike, so acting on rumours of gold, they set out for Macmillan River. They sold what was left of their horses and dogs at Fort Selkirk and canoed upstream against the spring flood, a trip that was perhaps more arduous than the winter trekking through the pass. After all their risks and adventures, Fraser and his friends never did find the gold they were looking for.

The pious and respected Fraser returned to a quiet life with his family as Government Agent for Atlin on July 1, 1902 and stayed in the post for 20 years. He earned $175 a month, the highest salary of any Government Agent at the time and an indication of how busy the mining business was there.

Fraser later wrote a diary of the eight months of his epic journey, which was passed down to his granddaughter, Gabriola Island's Sandy Duncan, author of 10 books. She wrote a novel, Gold Rush Orphan, which dramatizes her grandfather's odyssey. Each chapter begins with one of Fraser's diary entries, after which Duncan creates her fiction.

The Famous Gold Brick Robbery

Not only were Government Agents originally required to ship money to Victoria, but they also sent gold bars from mining communities to faraway places such as San Francisco. One such shipment went astray and led to a robbery, a Pinkerton Detective Agency search, and an old-fashioned, horseback murder.

On August 18, 1896, George McAuley, co-owner of Cariboo Amelia Mine, left Camp McKinney for San Francisco with 656 ounces of gold bars. This shipment, like all shipments, was supposed to be a highly guarded secret. Unfortunately, as reported in the Grand Forks Miner, "These Shipments have been made regularly for months past, and the public always knew within a day or two of the exact time at which it would pass through."

McAuley was robbed three miles away from Camp McKinney, at McMynn's Meadows (named after Government Agent William McMynn). When news of the crime reached camp, McAuley's partner, James Monahan, sent McAuley for the provincial police in Midway and organized a posse to search the area. They found nothing.

Cariboo Amelia Mine posted a $2,000 reward for the arrest and conviction of the robbers and an additional $1,500 for the recovery of the bullion.

Monahan discovered that a man named Matthew Roderick had been employed by the mine and on the day of the robbery had been absent from work. Several days later he had quit his job citing the need to return to his Seattle home. The miners in the camp, feeling sorry for him, had contributed $84 for his passage home, and away he went.

Convinced that Roderick was his man, Monahan hired a Pinkerton Agency detective who learned that, since returning from British Columbia, Roderick had paid up some back taxes and taken out a $3,000 insurance policy, a neat trick for a man who had left Camp McKinney under the charity of the miners. The detective surmised that Roderick had only managed to smuggle out the smaller of the three gold bars and that two must still be somewhere around Camp McKinney.

Roderick rode north for British Columbia, the Pinkerton agent following secretly behind. Word had reached the camp that he was on his way, and this time the men were ready for him. On October 26, 1896, Roderick approached the camp. Several of the men from camp, constables Cuppage and Dean, and Superintendent Keane, intercepted him.

After a brief silence, gunshots rang out. In his statement Dean said that "fearing Roderick had felled Keane, [he] fired his rifle at a dark figure of a man he had glimpsed in the flash of the preceding shot." He need not have fired his weapon though, because Keane's bullet had already killed Roderick. Dean had fired at the already dead, but falling, body of Matthew Roderick.

Here the story takes some interesting twists. Roderick's rifle, which Keane would later testify had been aimed at him, was actually found with a rag stuffed in the muzzle, and Roderick's pistol was covered in rust, indications that they had just been unearthed. An examination of Roderick's body showed he was wearing a special vest with a pocket under each armpit, large enough for each to accommodate a large gold bar. But there was no sign of gold.

A coroner's inquest into Roderick's death, held at Camp McKinney on November 11, 1896, found it a case of "justifiable homicide" and exonerated Keane of all blame. In a subsequent trial in Vernon in June 1897, he was found guilty, sentenced to one day in jail and released because he had already served it.

1878-1887
Government Agents first become appointed immigrant agents and officers and government recorders.

Camp McKinney was deserted long ago, and some say even the ghosts have gone. A trip up the road from Rock Creek reveals only a few piles of decaying timbers with perhaps a few original cabins refusing to fall down. But buried somewhere are two gold bars never recovered worth about US$220,000 in today's market.

THOSE THIRSTY PROSPECTORS

Then and now, Government Agents have garnered revenues from a wide range of services. Squirrelled away in the depths of the archives is a document the Lytton Government Agent sent to the colonial governor in 1864. It is an estimate of public revenue for 1865 based on Lytton's previous year's revenue (see the table below).

Next to the huge levy from road tolls, spirit licences earned considerably more revenue than any other category, including land registry and mining and trading licences. It seems those prospectors were very thirsty!

Earnings in 1865 and in Recent British Pound and Canadian Dollar Equivalents

Trading Licences	£235 THEN	=	£129,388.80 RECENT	=	CAD$290,622.69
Mining Licences	£160 THEN	=	£88,094.50 RECENT	=	CAD$197,866.92
General Mining Receipts	£150 THEN	=	£82,588.60 RECENT	=	CAD$185,492.32
Fines and Forfeitures	£90 THEN	=	£49,553.16 RECENT	=	CAD$111,295.39
Spirit Licences	£400 THEN	=	£220,236.26 RECENT	=	CAD$494,629.47
Land Revenue	£50 THEN	=	£27,529.53 RECENT	=	CAD$61,837.76
Land Registry	£5 THEN	=	£2,752.95 RECENT	=	CAD$6,183.77
Rents Exclusive of Lands	£140 THEN	=	£77,082.69 RECENT	=	CAD$173,124.66
Land Sales	£50 THEN	=	£27,529.53 RECENT	=	CAD$61,834.74
Road Tolls	£5,500 THEN	=	£3,028,248.53 RECENT	=	CAD$6,801,821.69

A PIECE OF CHILLIWACK HISTORY

Although the Government Agent office in Chilliwack, established in the early 1970s, is an infant in terms of Government Agent offices, it sits close to two points of historical importance: the Fraser River and the gold rush trail.

After gold ran out in the Cariboo, many settlers turned to farming and moved into Chilliwack and the surrounding area. The community of Columbia Valley lies adjacent to the southern end of Cultus Lake, and the Canada-U.S. border runs right through the valley.

In 1887, when the first families began arriving in Columbia Valley, many actually thought they were settling in the United States. Poor roads meant that valley residents remained oriented to that country until the Second World War, when access to it was greatly restricted.

The Jarabek, Minnick, Kosiker, and Dorko families were the first to settle in the valley. A school was erected on land adjacent to property owned by the Dorkos. The owner of the property on which the school was erected would not let the Dorko children cut across his property to the school, forcing them to take a longer route. Mysteriously one evening the school burned down, and when asked none of the Dorkos knew what had happened. The Dorkos built a new school on their land, which stood till around 1985.

The present-day Government Agent in Chilliwack is married to a descendant of the Dorkos.

1879
Government Agent John Tennant Ussher from Kamloops is killed in the line of duty, and a $1,000 reward is issued.

⊸ Wearing Many Hats ⊸

*A*S THE ONLY PERSON IN TOWN WITH LEGISLATED AUTHORITY, the first Government Agents "wore the hat" of whatever job needed to be done. So they might become a community's judge and tax collector and school inspector, all rolled into one. Even today a Government Agent might go by several other job titles as well such as notary public and office manager.

TALK ABOUT MULTI-TASKING

For the first 118 years of British Columbia's history, Government Agents were rugged men who performed many different duties in the colony's and, later, province's legal system. They often worked alone as the only provincial government representative in town. Those who were not strong as an ox, who could not manage money, treat people with honesty and patience, and handle a gun did not last long. They had to expect to be asked to do anything-and often were.

Government Agents used whichever job title that would garner them the desired result for the function they were performing. In small, newly formed pioneer sites far from the capital city of Victoria, they frequently acted in a breathtaking array of portfolios: sheriff, hangman, mayor, city planner, justice of the peace, Crown prosecutor, county court judge, gold commissioner, Indian agent, school inspector, collector of road taxes, provincial collector, coroner, registrar of voters, local assistant to the fire commissioner, water recorder, official administrator, assistant commissioner of lands and works, and collector of revenue. Although there was no official name for it, they even watched out for the sick and destitute in their districts.

These appointments gave Government Agents the opportunity to take a constant pulse of the underbelly of their communities. It also allowed them to witness some interesting rulings during the early development of the province.

As collector of voters, or what is now called the registrar of voters, Government Agents had to abide by one 1898 regulation that would never be acceptable today: they were fined $50 for the "name of every Chinaman, Japanese, or Indian" that appeared on the voters list. Women were also barred from the list, as they were not recognized as persons under the law.

THE STORY OF WON ALEXANDER CUMYOW

The life of Won Alexander Cumyow (温金有; pinyin: Wēn Jīnyǒu) has many interesting moments of intersection with that of the Government Agents organization. Won Alexander Cumyow (温金有; pinyin: Wēn Jīnyǒu) was born on February 14, 1861 (it could be March 24 depending on the calendar used) in Port Douglas, British Columbia. Port Douglas was at the start of the Douglas Road to Lillooet, constructed for the flow of goods and miners to the Fraser River Gold Rush. Won Alexander Cumyow (温金有; pinyin: Wēn Jīnyǒu)) was the oldest son of Won Lin Ling, a store and restaurant owner who had emigrated in 1858 from Canton, China to San Francisco and later to Port Douglas. Won Alexander Cumyow (温金有; pinyin: Wēn Jīnyǒu) was the first person of Chinese descent born in Canada. He was duly registered as a British Subject — thus the first time his path crossed with that of a Government Agent.

Won Alexander Cumyow (温金有; pinyin: Wēn Jīnyǒu) attended high school in New Westminster, studied law and articled but was not permitted a license. Things had changed in British Columbia from the time of his birth to the time he was ready to practise law. Some have argued it was economic conditions, some a clash of cultures and some have said politics. Whatever the reasons, British Columbia had moved away from James Douglas's vision of a multicultural society when the colony was founded in 1858 to one that started to invoke laws that discriminated based on race.

By 1875, provincial legislation was passed which took the franchise away from Chinese-Canadians and First Nations people. The legislation would not apply however, to Won Alexander Cumyow (温金有; pinyin: Wēn Jīnyǒu) when he became legal voting age.

Paths crossed again in 1881 when Governemt Agents, wearing another hat, were involved in the census and reconnected with Won Alexander Cumyow (温金有; pinyin: Wēn Jīnyǒu) as his family's particulars were recorded.

DIRECTLY TO THE PREMIER

Even after decades of settlement, the British Columbia civil service remained rather small, although Government Agents comprised a good portion of it. In 1871, 22 out of 60 civil servants were Government Agents and their staff. Twenty years later the number doubled: 44 out of 109 civil servants were Government Agents and staff. Hence they could correspond directly with the premier of the day.

A theoretical pairing of the real-life things they were asked to do 100 or so years ago with the government departments of today might look like this:

1880
The appointment of a Deputy Government Agent appears for the first time at the New Westminster office.

- **Queen's Printer**: in 1897, the Revelstoke Government Agent's write-ups of mining camps in the Kootenay Mail were reproduced for government at 5½ per copy.

- **BC Statistics**: in 1897, Government Agents were asked to conduct a survey on business in their areas for statistics.

- **Economic Development**: in 1904, W.W.B. McInnes, MPP, enclosed some correspondence to the premier and suggested that something should be done about H. Carmichael, a government official, recommending that the capitalists not go to Alberni.

- **Health Authorities**: in 1900, the Government Agent in Atlin was involved with the Presbyterian hospital and payment for the care of indigents.

- **Industrial Inquiry Commissioner**: in 1910, an agent reported that if the Esquimalt and Nanaimo Railway was prepared to pay the prevailing local wage rate, it would have no difficulty procuring labourers.

- **Provincial Emergency Program**: in 1910, the Acting Government Agent at Golden acknowledged a telegram authorizing him to render assistance in a disaster at Rogers Pass.

- **Protocol and Intergovernment Relations**: in 1910, the Prince Rupert agent sought approval for an expenditure to decorate the government buildings for a visit from then Prime Minister Laurier.

- **Public Works**: in 1900, the Government Agent at Cumberland was instructed to build a new wharf on Hornby Island.

- **Workers Compensation Board**: in 1909, H.C. Rayson, Alberni's Government Agent, reported on the claim that H. Varney was injured by falling rock from blasting operations at Quatsino.

Serving a Search Warrant on Yourself

How many times have Government Agents, by virtue of the many hats they have worn, had to issue a search warrant on themselves? It has happened.

In the 1970s, Robert Hall served as, among other things, Government Agent in the branch's most northern outpost of Atlin. In 1978, the RCMP arrived from Yukon and served Hall, who was also the mining recorder, a search warrant for mining papers regarding an investigation into the activities of some less than stellar Yukon residents.

The RCMP officers then asked the court clerk where they could find a justice of the peace; their document, which had been prepared in the Yukon, had to be signed off by a member of the British Columbia judicial system. The officers then appeared before His Honour Justice of the Peace Hall, who checked to see that the documents were in order, took the oath required, and signed off on the search warrant.

The officers then asked Justice Hall where the mining recorder's office was. He pointed to a building behind the courthouse and said the mining recorder would not be in until later in the day after court had adjourned.

Later that afternoon the RCMP entered the Government Agent office and asked to speak to the mining recorder. The clerk directed them to Hall — the all-in-one Government Agent, justice of the peace, and mining recorder. The RCMP then served Mining Recorder Hall the same search warrant he had authorized himself just a few hours earlier.

In the Line of Duty

During the colonial period, gold commissioners were sometimes appointed customs officers. Captain H.O. Travaillot, a French master mariner, was one who performed both duties at the Forks (known today as Lytton) from 1858 to 1859.

In the winter of 1858, Travaillot seized a pack train of contraband liquor. A group of prospectors heard about the seizure, and one of them, James Glennon, suggested that as a matter of courtesy they should all pay their respects to the gold commissioner. When the group arrived at Travaillot's quarters, he invited them to come in and sit down where it was warm. Glennon and Travaillot did the talking while the others sat back and listened. Then there came a pause in the conversation.

"Captain," said Glennon, "it is reported in town that a great joke has been played on you: it is said that those kegs of liquor you seized were filled with water!"

Travaillot's reaction was both immediate and dramatic. He invited Glennon to bring forward a keg, any keg, from the contraband so that it could be tapped and tested, and the affront to his dignity and professional competence erased. One was duly brought in and tapped, and a glass of its contents was drawn off. Travaillot passed the glass to Glennon, who sampled it and agreed that, yes, it certainly was liquor, and quite palatable liquor at that.

Since the keg had been opened and since there were several thirsty prospectors and one thirsty gold commissioner in the room, a sampling of the keg's contents seemed called for. Travaillot, not one to forget his duty as host, took part with such enthusiasm that the prospectors had to put him to bed.

1883
Government Agents are appointed as jury selectors.

WILD HORSE BOUNTIES

Another task of early Government Agents was to issue grazing leases and bounty money for wild horses, of which there were a great many. In the Kootenays in particular, an estimated 2,500 to 5,000 of them roamed the countryside.

People believed the animals competed with domestic horses for grazing and that they carried transmittable diseases. As well, the colonial government recognized that ranchers needed other opportunities to sustain themselves, so a formal plan to eliminate wild horses was created. Once the horses were disposed of, more grazing permits to specific areas were awarded to the ranchers.

Of course it fell to the Government Agents to decide how much bounty to pay for the wild horses. But how were the horses delivered to them? Very creatively, according to government records of the time: "Many of the horses were shot and left to rot on the range, and many were shipped away for fox meat. Some people removed the horses' manes and tails and sold them for furniture stuffing.... The ears were sliced off, still connected at the scalp, and turned in to the government agent for bounty money."

Thankfully, Government Agents do not have to deal with horse bounties today!

The Lytton stage coach consisted of an open, buckboard wagon and just two horses.

SITTING ON THE FENCE

One of the stranger duties that Government Agents performed in the early days of the province, before land surveys were readily available, was that of fence viewer. They appear to have carried out this job until some time in the 1950s when the B.C. Ministry of Agriculture began using its own staff and contractors.

Actual legislation for fence viewing existed originally in the Line Fences Act, which provided for the appointment of fence viewers in "unorganized territory" to resolve the quality, nature, and location of a fence and whether it did or did not need repair. Any landowner who wanted to mark the boundary between their land and someone else's with a fence, or who already owned a fence and wanted to have it repaired, had to notify either a minister of the government or the local Government Agent to come and "view" the fence. The fence viewer would help make the decision about the fence. Landowners were not necessarily farmers and ranchers, although they did require fence viewers, but were also members of industry and owners of recreational properties.

It sounds rather pastoral, but in fact was not, as neighbours often got into nasty squabbles that even impartial fence viewers, try as they might, found difficult to resolve.

In 1971, after much debate in the B.C. legislature, Bill 23 replaced the Line Fences Act, because it was becoming increasingly difficult to get fence viewers.

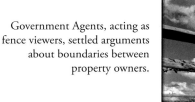

Government Agents, acting as fence viewers, settled arguments about boundaries between property owners.

PRO HOCKEY PLAYER TURNED GOVERNMENT AGENT

While Government Agents have juggled various duties during their careers, few can say they have had the privilege of balancing a job in government with one in the National Hockey League.

Henry Spencer Tatchell, or Spence as he was known to his friends and colleagues, for years played professional hockey while he held down a government post. His career in the civil service included Government Agent positions in Nelson, Cranbrook,

1885
Government Agents are appointed as Chinese collectors as per the Chinese Regulation Act of 1884.

Merritt, Salmon Arm, and Quesnel from the 1940s to his retirement as regional provincial district manager for the Kootenay agencies in 1984.

Tatchell launched a successful professional career in hockey in Winnipeg, Manitoba in 1940. He played for the New York Rangers in 1942-43. On April 15, 1943, Tatchell joined the Royal Canadian Navy in Winnipeg and, while in training, played for the Cornwallis Navy.

After World War II, Tatchell played for the Nelson Maple Leafs of the Kootenay League for five years. After several seasons with the Kimberley Dynamiters in the Kootenay and in the WIHL, he retired from hockey but continued his career with the provincial government. He is listed in the NHL Players Association's Legends of Hockey section.

In later life Tatchell described his decision to leave hockey in a letter he wrote in the 1990s:

> "I can't resist telling you another tale that was a big turning point in our lives. At the precise time (9:00 am on September 16, 1946) that I started work with the government in Nelson, Mr. Hamilton, the Government Agent at the time, took me into his office because there was a phone call for me from Buffalo, NY. He left closing the door. The gentleman on the telephone told me I had been traded from NY to Buffalo during the war. After a report from the guy that had scouted me in the spring of 1946, he wanted me to play for them, for the salary of $2,500.00. Good remuneration for the time, but I decided on the spot that I had a good shot at a career job for life with the government. He was a nice man from Winnipeg and said to call him if I changed my mind. The thing that seems so 'magical' for us was the timing...to the second."

Tatchell's children once asked him if he had ever regretted his decision to become a Government Agent rather than continue his career in the NHL. He announced that he had not.

The Man with Many Hats

Just as Robert Hall was Government Agent, justice of the peace, and mining recorder all rolled into one and wound up serving himself a search warrant, other staff have found themselves in precarious situations in which they have had to wear more than one hat on one occasion. One agent took it to a whole new level by "switching hats" more than five times.

Back in the Cariboo gold rush days, two thirsty and tired prospectors sought accommodation and liquid refreshment after a long sojourn in the hills. The local Government Agent issued them liquor permits, and then, as liquor vendor, sold them a supply, which they took back to their hotel.

The prospectors had quenched their thirst later that day. As the local provincial constable, the Government Agent put them in jail to dry out. As the provincial gaoler, he cared for them overnight. As stipendiary magistrate, he judged the prospectors guilty the next day and gave them a fine. As clerk of the peace, he received their fine, and as Government Agent he transferred the funds to the provincial Treasury.

1889
The appointment of a Government Agent clerk first appears at the New Westminster office.

Taking Matters into Their Own Hands

SOMETIMES THE USUAL RULES AND REGULATIONS just do not seem to fit. Then again, sometimes the requests are so unusual that Government Agents have to be creative and take matters into their own hands.

HE DID IT HIS WAY

James Spalding began his current job as Ucluelet Government Agent in August 1988. He describes the office as it was when he joined and his predecessor, who became a good friend and who had his own way of doing things:

> "While Joe Stanhope was Government Agent in Ucluelet, the office, which had been in the same location since 1974, consisted of one small room with a washroom in the rear corner. A Jack Russell Terrier named Pepper that belonged to the notary public next door wandered into the office on numerous occasions and made himself comfortable in the Government Agent's chair.
>
> "Joe was not the most organized Government Agent in the province at that time- or so it appeared. The office consisted of two desks behind the counter, one for the Government Agent and one that was used as a cash-out and stock area. Joe had been hired from outside government, so he was unfamiliar with its filing system.
>
> "What really grabbed my attention were the numerous piles of paper on the side of the front counter, on Joe's desk, and on the cash-out desk. These stacks of paper appeared to be memos, bulletins, letters, and various other documents. Each pile was between six inches and over a foot in height.
>
> "I never was privileged enough to see Joe in action, but many of the old-timers in the community were absolutely amazed by Joe's technique. Apparently when a customer came to the office on provincial business, if Joe did not know the answer, he would immediately go to one of these many stacks of forms, begin to furiously flip through them, and in a matter of seconds or minutes, find the exact memo required for the customer.
>
> "It is just too bad that video cameras were not widely used dur-

ing this period, because a video of Joe in action would have been astounding, I am sure."

SQUEEZING IN THE LAST CUSTOMER

Vancouver's Government Agent office moved several times before closing its doors in 1983, but not without serving its very last customer at the very last possible moment.

The city's first permanent Government Agent office opened in 1911-although Vancouver had maintained, in conjunction with New Westminster, a constable and Government Agent since 1871-at the intersection of Pender and Richards streets. It eventually moved to the magnificent Vancouver courthouse, (now the Vancouver Art Gallery).

The office moved a third time, to 535 Burrard Street, close to the Bentall Centre, but the building was demolished and the site incorporated into a city park.

In 1978, the office relocated for the fourth and final time to Room 222 in Robson Square. Peter Block, the Government Agent at the time, had played such an important role in setting up the new administration centre that he was known as the "Uncrowned King of Robson Square."

One intriguing role played by the Vancouver Government Agent office was that of test bed for new technologies or procedures. The former Telecommunications Branch installed one of the first two high-speed FAXs in the office in February 1982 (the other was installed in the Victoria Message Centre). Other offices were encouraged to use the FAX machine and to experiment and discover how this new communication tool could work for them.

In the mid-1980s, the Vancouver office tested the first phase of the current provincial 1-800 telephone system for long-distance calls. It was also responsible for maintaining a Telidon terminal (Telidon was a Canadian second-generation videotext system-literally the Internet before its time).

Nonetheless, the Vancouver Government Agent office closed its doors to the public on August 31, 1983. On that day, just as staff were locking up for the last time, the late Davie Fulton, MP for Kamloops, former federal minister of justice in the Diefenbaker government, and former Supreme Court Justice, appeared. He had come for his B.C. resident hunter's number, only to find the office doors closed. The switchboard operator at the building's front reception desk had sent him to the back entrance of the office to ask what could be done. Luckily, staff were able to assist Fulton, who was most grateful. The staff would not have it any other way.

1891
Government Agent Stephen Hussey from Kamloops becomes the superintendent of the B.C. provincial police and moves to Victoria. Government Agents are appointed as assessors and collectors of provincial revenue.

Giving and Receiving

In the mid-1980s, the Alaska Marine Highway System had its doubts about the port of Prince Rupert. A series of disputes and protests had led to the blocking of its ferry. A meeting was held in Hyder, Alaska to examine the feasibility of extending the marine highway system out to other communities to possibly replace Prince Rupert. The residents of Stewart, B.C. were invited.

The Alaska government had one problem though. Its cash flow from the rich oil fields was dwindling, and the state had no funds to build a terminal in Hyder, which would run from

$5 million to $6 million (in those days around CAD$10 million) for only 86 citizens. The Canadians on the other side of the border could not be counted in the calculation for the expenditure of state funds.

The governor of Alaska, however, thinking that 86 people would not be able to raise millions of dollars, said that if the community of Stewart came up with a terminal, the weekly ferry service would be put in place there. He could not have known that a young Government Agent and a pharmacist turned mayor had a plan.

The city of Stewart has deep water close to shore and a federal dock that can take the whole length of a marine vessel. The trick was to get the cars off and the residents safely into Hyder, as the border crossing had been closed and the customs house removed.

The two carried out their plan. They dumped rock into the channel to form a breakwater, to which was attached an Akron bridge borrowed from the Ministry of Highways. It pivoted on one end and had rollers on the other, and the rollers travelled across the deck of a barge from Arrow Transportation Systems, rented for $1 per year. From the rear of the ferry a car could drive onto the barge, up the Akron bridge, now a ramp, across the breakwater and onto the highway.

After five months the governor was informed that his ferry dock was ready. It cost only CAD$50,000. But one last glitch remained: some items were legal in Alaska but illegal in Canada. Therefore, the ferry would come in at 10:00 a.m., land would be ceded to the United States, and at 2:00 p.m. it would be returned to Canada. It just so happened that the B.C. Government Agent handled court matters for both the State of Alaska and the Province of British Columbia.

This actually did work for awhile, until someone discovered that land could only be ceded by an act of parliament and an act of congress, which was undesirable for a variety of reasons. So after several months of giving and receiving territory each Friday, the Government Agent put down his pen and the border stopped its dance. Eventually the ferry stopped running altogether.

A True Scot

Colourful stories abound about one of British Columbia's most bearded and bushy Government Agents, Walter Scott.

Born in Dumfriesshire, Scotland in 1847, he immigrated to Canada in 1887. After a brief stint as a farmer and then prospector, Scott became mining recorder for the Illecillewaet Mining Division. He and his wife moved to Nakusp in 1899, and he became mining recorder and constable there in 1901. Eventually he was promoted to Government Agent when the agency office was opened in 1913, a position he held until he was 83 or, possibly, 87, giving him the distinction of being the oldest Government Agent.

Although he loved British Columbia, the man never lost the affection he felt for his homeland roots. One imagines he spoke with a good Scottish burr all his life-and that he never forgot even the smallest debt. One wintery day in 1907, Scott asked his friend Bert Herridge to shovel the snow off his verandah. When the job was done, Scott said, "Many thanks, Herbie. I'll repay thee some day."

No less than 12 years later, in the spring of 1919, Herridge took a document to Scott to be witnessed. When Herridge asked him what he owed for the service, Walter said, "My fee is 50 cents." Then he went on to say, "Do ye ken the day when ye shovelled the verandah and I promised to repay thee some day? Well, Herbie, we are quits!"

Scott took that frugality a step further the day he took a package for his brother in Australia to the Nakusp post office. Postage turned out to be more than he had expected. In fact, it was one cent more than he had expected. But he knew what to do: to the postmaster he said, "Gie me the bundle back. I'll tak' it hame and cut out the advairtisements!"

Of course, Scott was known to favour an occasional dram of whiskey to "ward off the chill." During British Columbia's brief experimentation with prohibition between 1917 and 1921, Government Agents served as liquor vendors. Alcohol was only available for medicinal or sacramental purposes, and a good number of prescriptions were written up for conditions which, oddly enough, could only be treated by the internal application of spirits. Prescription in hand, the patient then visited their Government Agent, who would dispense the curative potion.

1899
Small debts court and fence viewer appointments.

In 1921, when the plebiscite on the repeal of prohibition was held, Scott and his same friend Herridge were responsible for counting the Nakusp ballots. The ballots were counted once, then twice, and each time a tie resulted. Scott became agitated. Herridge examined the ballot box and found a single ballot wedged between the joints. It was a vote for repeal.

Government Agent Walter Scott.

Scott could contain himself no longer. He threw up his arms and shouted, "Praise the Lord, Praise the Lord, John Barleycorn has won!" It is probably safe to assume that Walter Scott had reservations on the subject of prohibition.

Scott died in Nakusp in 1936. He and his wife are buried in the Revelstoke cemetery.

Solving Mineral Disputes with a Smith and Wesson

Sidney Russell Almond joined the government service in the summer of 1897 when he became mining recorder in Boundary country. In 1898, he was made Gold Commissioner and, in 1904, Government Agent.

Almond wrote his memoirs in August 1930, after his retirement. At one point, he mentions Gold Commissioner William McMynn. Being Chief Constable as well as Gold Commissioner and Government Agent may have cut him considerable latitude in dealing with the two gentlemen who were disturbing the peace:

> "There was a great rush of prospectors to the Mining Recorder's office when I opened it in 1897. I would have no time to keep my work up during the day, attending to people at the counter, and so I would be up every night until two o'clock in the morning to get the work done.
>
> "I had twenty-seven claims recorded in one day. There was not only

the time taken up with each case at the counter but there was all the office work in connection with each which had to be attended to afterwards. There was a lot done in the way of speculators buying up prospects and selling them at a good profit, and prospectors locating a claim and selling it for a couple of hundred dollars. All these transfers had to be recorded.

"Sometimes prospectors would knock you up in the middle of the night to get a claim recorded to get ahead of somebody else, not realizing that you could not deal with them except during business hours. But they wakened you up and by the time you got through explaining that they would have to come back at nine o'clock in the morning, you were wide awake for the rest of the night. McMynn shot two men that were waiting on his doorstep one night and raising a dickens of a row, waiting to record the same claim. He caught one fellow in the leg. They were arguing on the doorstep as to who staked first and each wanting McMynn to take his story as the true one. McMynn lived upstairs in the same building where he had his office."

It is not known what became of the prospectors.

Full Circle

The brutal murder of one Government Agent staff lay forgotten for more than 100 years until his remains were accidentally rediscovered in 1987. Then a present-day agent took the matter into his own hands.

In July 1882, Enderby's Government Agent, T.M. Lambly, hired prospector Aeneas Dewar to collect the poll tax from miners working at Cherry Creek. After Dewar had collected the taxes, which amounted to about $30, he had dinner at the cabin of his acquaintance, Smart Aleck. But when Dewar's horse was found later wandering without a rider, suspicions arose. Twenty days afterward, Dewar's body was found buried under Smart Aleck's cabin-and was left there, for some reason. He had died of a violent axe blow to the back of his head. Despite a lucrative $1,000 reward the murderer was never found and the reward never claimed.

One hundred and five years later, on May 11, 1987, while working on a mineral claim, a backhoe operator uncovered human bones near Cherryville, B.C. The bones were located in an area under an old prospector's cabin, buried four to five feet below ground level. The skull had a large cut on the back. The holder of the mineral claim

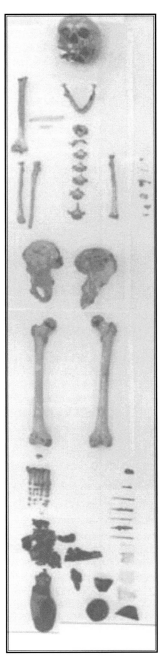

recalled a story about a poll tax collector who was killed back in the 1880s by a miner known as Smart Aleck.

The bones were taken to Norm Schultz, the coroner at the time (who was to be the last Government Agent/coroner in the Okanagan), to confirm their identity. Wanting to ensure the trail of evidence was not compromised by leaving the bones unaccounted for, he did what any Government Agent would have done: he took them home from the excavation site and carefully placed them on the dining room table. It appears that Schultz's wife was not as impressed with the find as he was, and they quickly found a new place to keep the bones prior to turning them over to the hospital pathology lab.

Left
Murdered Government Agent staff Aeneas Dewar.

Far Left
The bones of Aeneas Dewar that Coroner Norm Schultz examined on his dining room table.

RAISING A RUCKUS OVER THE FLAG—OR LACK THEREOF

The pen is mightier than the sword-and one should not do battle with someone who buys ink by the gallon. One gold commissioner found this out the hard way.

An incident in early July 1899 drew the ire of an entire town and prompted an article in The Prospector. Lillooet's Gold Commissioner Frederick Soues, who "never misses a chance to put in a word against Canada and Canadians and to express his opinions of the government which employs him," reported the paper, seems not to have been on very good standing with many of the townsfolk of Clinton.

On Dominion Day that year Soues refused to fly the flag at the Clinton government buildings. Why? He said it was because he had received no official notice of the day or orders to put the flag up. Taking matters into their own hands, someone that evening cut the pole down. Not to be outdone, Soues viewed the remains of the pole and then completely obliterated all of the evidence.

"As to receiving official notice to have the flag up," said The Prospector, "it no doubt was for political reasons as he wished to impress people of the large amount of work and red tape necessary in his office since the new government came into power. The Government should send him official notice at once that would bring him to his senses, if he has any."

Since 1900 at least, the standard practice is for the protocol office provincially or federally to issue notices regarding the raising and lowering of flags. Perhaps this event is what set the practice in motion.

Gold Commissioner Fred Soues.

1917-1921
During the prohibition years, Government Agents serve as liquor vendors, as the sale of liquor is restricted to medicinal, scientific, or sacramental purposes.

The Dream of Chartres Brew

From the earliest stories of colonial life the name of one of the great pioneers of British Columbia appears over and over again. Whenever there was a mess to clean up during the Cariboo gold rush, more often than not, Chartres Brew was there to do it. He was a man with a dream.

Noted for his courage, temper, wit, and integrity as well as bravery in the Crimean War, Brew was solicited in 1858 by Sir Edward Bulwer-Lytton to be the chief inspector of police for the new Colony of British Columbia. Brew accepted the call, came to B.C. (surviving a shipwreck on the way from England) and surveyed the situation. He immediately asked for a police force of 150 men. He wanted them to be trained and equipped locally, organized along military lines, and centrally controlled. Brew never lived to see this dream fulfilled. Governor Douglas doubted the wisdom of recruiting police from a mining population that included so many Americans and requested that 60 members of the Irish constabulary be sent to form a nucleus (one of whom was Gold Commissioner Thomas Elwyn).

Brew was often sent to the middle of skirmishes to apply his skills. In January 1859, a bitter dispute erupted between the justice of the peace at Hills Bar and the gold commissioner at Yale. The notorious Ned McGowan, a vigilante on the run from California, was organizing his followers at Yale to fight against the authorities. Douglas appointed Brew the chief gold commissioner and sent him and three constables to Yale to quell McGowan. Troubles subsided, and Brew recommended the establishment there of a force of 20 constables, because the constables that had been recruited from among the miners by the former gold commissioner, he reported, were "nearly all a worthless set of loungers." Later 80 miners paid tribute to his ability to give justice while keeping "the kind feelings and respect of all."

Brew now thought 150 Irish constabulary should be obtained for the colony-and this time Douglas concurred. However, when the cost was made clear and the British government refused to bear the expense, the plan was again dropped.

In 1864, fearing an Indian uprising after the Bute Inlet attack, Brew led a daring expedition into the interior plains to apprehend the murderers. His party had to cross the Cascade Mountains and make a 250-mile march to Puntzi Lake.

Brew never got the police force he had dreamed of. Yet Governors Douglas and Seymour regarded him as without equal in the role of gold commissioner and stipendiary magistrate. He established a standard of conduct that maintained peace in the gold fields at the height of their production with no more than 18 constables in regular employment.

1920
The first mention of the appointment of Government Agents as commissioners for taking affidavits.

1920s
Government Agents appointed as school tax assessors.

Plates

Peter Rodseth's carving in the
Vanderhoof Service BC Centre.

Proclamation

By His Excellency James Douglas Governor of Vancouver's Island and its Dependencies

Whereas by law all mines of gold, and all gold in its natural place of deposit within the districts of Frasers River and of Thompson's River commonly known as the Couteau, Coutreau and Shuswap countries whether on the lands of the Queen or any of Her Majesty's Subjects, belong to the Crown.

And whereas information has been received by the Government that gold exists upon, and in the soil of the said districts, and that certain persons have commenced or are about to commence searching and digging for the same for their own use, without leave or other authority from Her Majesty.

Now I James Douglas the Governor aforesaid in behalf of Her Majesty do hereby publickly notify and declare that all persons who shall take from any lands within the said districts, any gold, metal or ore containing gold, or who shall dig for and disturb the soil in search of gold, metal or ore, without having been duly authorized in that behalf by Her Majesty's Colonial Government will be prosecuted both criminally and civilly as the law allows.

And I further notify and declare such regulations as may [...] appointed [...] the terms [...]

for this purpose, on the payment of a reasonable fee.

Given under my hand and Seal at the Government Office, Victoria, this twenty eighth day of December in the year of Our Lord One thousand eight hundred and fifty seven, and in the twenty first year of Her Majesty's reign

*Signed, James Douglas
Governor.*

*By His Excellency's Command
Richard Golledge
Secretary*

God Save the Queen

Governor James Douglas's proclamation, dated December 28, 1857, that all of the gold in the districts of the Fraser and Thompson rivers belongs to the Crown.

Government Office Victoria
30th December 1858

With reference to the Proclamation issued on the 28th of December, declaring the rights of the Crown in respect to gold found in its natural place of deposit within the Districts of Fraser River and of Thompson River, commonly known as the Quatton, Couteau and Shuswap — and their ——

His Excellency the Governor has been pleased to establish the following additional regulations under which Licenses may be obtained to dig, search for and remove the ——

1st. From and after the first day of February next no person will be permitted to dig, search for or remove gold on or from any lands, public or private, without first taking out and keeping up for a License in the form ——

2nd. For the present and for the —— sale ——— of the cover and private —— of the said deposits, the License fee is now fixed at Twenty one shillings per month to be paid in advance, but it is to ——— that the rate as such may be —— withdrawn or altered ——

3rd. ——

4th. Rules adjusting the extent and position of land to be covered by each licence and for the prevention of confusion, and the interference of one licence with another will be regulated by the said Commissioner.

Signed James Douglas
Governor,

By His Excellency's command
Richard Golledge,
Secretary

God Save the Queen

Form of Gold Licence

No   185

The Bearer
having paid to me the sum of Twenty one
shillings on account of the Territorial Revenue,
I hereby licence him to dig search for and
remove gold on and from any such Crown
land within the
as I shall assign to him for that purpose
during the month of   185
This Licence must be produced whenever
demanded by me or any person acting
under the authority of the Government.

Signed
Commissioner

Governor Douglas writes a letter regarding the proclamation he wrote three days earlier.

Governor Douglas issues instructions to an assistant gold commissioner on July 1, 1858.

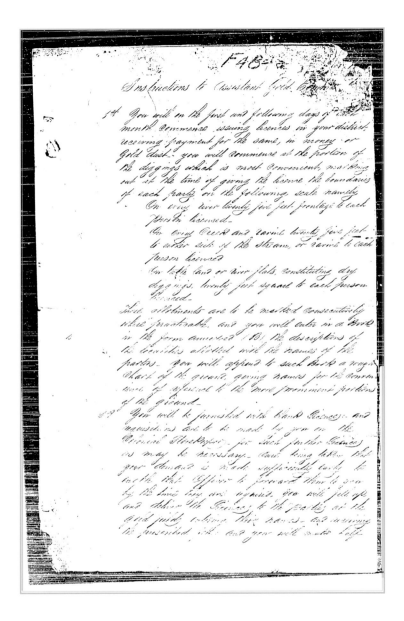

Provincial Leaders 1858–2008

GOVERNORS OF BRITISH COLUMBIA	TERM
Sir James Douglas	1858–1864
Frederick Seymour	1864–1866

GOVERNORS OF THE UNITED COLONIES OF VANCOUVER ISLAND AND BRITISH COLUMBIA	TERM
Frederick Seymour	1866–1869
Sir Anthony Musgrave	1869–1871

PREMIERS OF BRITISH COLUMBIA	TERM
John Foster McCreight	1871–1874
Amor De Cosmos (William Alexander Smith)	1872–1874
George Anthony Boomer Walkem	1874–1876
Andrew Charles Elliott	1876–1878
George Anthony Boomer Walkem	1878–1882
Robert Beaven	1882–1883
William Smithe	1883–1887
Alexander Edmund Batson Davie	1887–1889
John Robson	1889–1892
Theodore Davie	1892–1895
John Herbert Turner	1895–1898
Charles Augustus Semlin	1898–1900
Joseph Martin	1900

BRITISH COLUMBIA

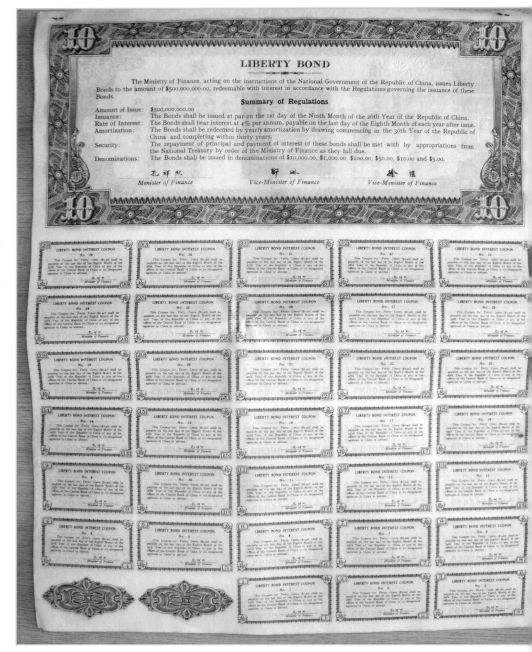

Chinese immigration to Canada began in 1858 with the gold rush. The Chinese brought bond coupons to Government Agent offices to be cashed.

The Cariboo stage,
Clinton, B.C., 1887.

Columbia Street,
New Westminster, in the 1880s.

Government buildings erected
in 1887 by A.C. Vowell,
Windermere's Government
Agent, at the north end of
Lake Windermere in the
Columbia Valley.

RANGERS ALL-TIME ROSTER

Spence
Tatchell
Defense

Birthdate: Jul. 16, 1924

Birthplace: Lloydminster, Saskatchewan

Hometown: Winnipeg, Manitoba

Height: 5'11"   **Weight:** 175 lbs.

17

Professional hockey player
and Government Agent
Spence Tatchell

The gold scale of
Deborah Lipscombe,
Regional Director and one of
the last Government Agent gold
commissioners in B.C.

Keeping Up the Momentum

FROM OFFICES IN LEFTOVER LIQUOR STORES to spaces adorned with hand-carved art, Government Agents work with the same dedication everywhere.

LOST THEN FOUND

Every so often staff are asked to do a general cleanup of secure storage areas, walk-in vaults in courthouses, safes in hallways, and mail rooms, and it is surprising what can be found lurking in those corners. It is also surprising what happens to that material after the Government Agent inventories the contents and ships it to Victoria for safekeeping or disposal.

During one routine "spring cleaning" in Victoria about 30 years ago, staff found a small box in a Ministry of Finance vault. A local locksmith was fetched to open it up, and lo and behold, a treasure lay sparkling: seven sizeable gold nuggets, several vials of platinum nuggets, high grade ore samples, and a rare 10 gram specimen of crystalline gold.

The box had lain forgotten in the vault for 50 years, since the B.C. government had purchased it in 1937 for $1,500. The largest gold piece, which was eight inches long and four inches wide and weighed 1,641 grams (more than three pounds) was identified as the Turnagain nugget, a gem of rare size and purity, named for the river in northern British Columbia in which it was found. It is believed to be the second largest gold nugget in British Columbia's history and would be worth more than a quarter of a million dollars on today's market.

GOVERNMENT AGENTS MIGHT LAUGH

Government Agents in 100 Mile House might laugh now to think of the town's first public office in November 1973. Government Agent Jim Dunsmuir rented 4,000 square feet of open space-namely, the old liquor store.

In the beginning, the office displayed half-inch plywood on sawhorses and part of the old liquor store counter. Staff's first winter in the building was a challenge, as they worked all day in heavy coats and boots to keep warm. Every time the door opened, they lost all the heat from the building, and it took hours to warm up. The windows had bars on them, a perfect setting for the first civil marriages.

Large cracks in the floor tripped up customers, and the old, exposed fluorescent lights blew up on several occasions, sending pieces of glass all over the room. Sometimes the gas coming from the tubes was so strong that everyone had to leave the building.

To operate the office machinery, staff ran adaptors from the four electrical outlets until the electrical inspector condemned the wiring. In the spring of 1974, the Department of Public Works arrived to repair the wiring and lighting. After they had added an inside entrance with a glass door, a customer walked right through it. Fortunately, he was not hurt, just a little surprised.

CONTINUALLY IMPROVING SERVICE DELIVERY

In 2002, Darlene Driediger became temporary Government Agent of Nakusp after the early retirement of Judy Young, who had held the position since 1974. One of Driediger's very first tasks was to investigate the possibility of combining the Government Agent office and staff with the Ministry of Employment and Income Assistance, and the Ministry of Children and Family Development into one working unit. With the co-operation of senior managers and a local working group the three ministries began working as one in May 2003.

One day in the first month of the newly combined ministries, several citizens came into the office for government services. One customer was looking for financial assistance to help him with his living expenses, another sought to file a new business name, and a third was paying his property taxes.

The office was fairly busy that day, and two other customers were already being serviced by the customer service representative and Driediger. As the counter customers were being helped, Driediger could not help but notice the interaction between the three men in the public waiting area: the taxpayer and the businessman were making their wait-time short with a lively conversation about the local hot spot for fishing Gerard Trout. Their fishing stories were descriptive and action filled.

As the two men were talking, the third customer, who normally would not have been in the same office as these two men nor talking with them on the street, came forward and joined the conversation. The businessman and the taxpayer were a little surprised at first to be approached by this individual "who was one of those people on welfare," but as he shared his own experiences with the mighty Gerard Trout, the conversation continued amongst all three men with all the excitement of a good fishing story. Staff found it heartwarming to see this mix of clientele interact without judgment of each other.

1922-23
R. Ross Napier appointed inspector of agencies and conducts the first provincial review of Government Agent offices.

Nakusp was one of the first Government Agent offices to offer combined services at the local community level. Many more offices, now called Service BC Centres, have followed suit and now deliver combined services, which are tailor-made to their communities.

FINDING A RESOLUTION

While citizen-centred service delivery is new to many government departments, it is something that Service BC has practised since its inception. And quite often Government Agents have had to balance what was legally correct with their own internal moral code of what was right and just. Finding a resolution was more important than finding blame. Proof of that commitment can be found in this letter dated August 9, 1939.

Government Agent C. Nichols was attempting to get a Mrs. Bromley, who was

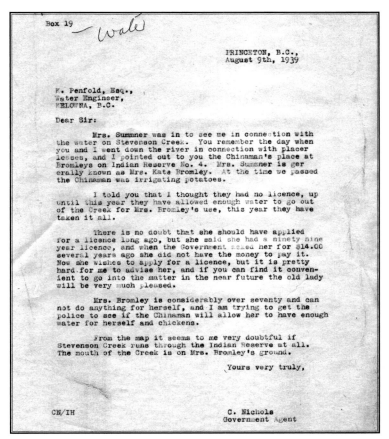

Government Agent C. Nichols works on behalf of one of his customers.

over 70 years old and had been unable to pay $14 for the 99-year lease on her water licence during the Depression, enough water for herself and her chickens. The creek near her house was drying up before it reached her property because of upstream use.

Up until the 1990s Government Agents were also water recorders, so it was not unusual for them to be involved in matters concerning water rights.

Giving Credit where Credit is Due

Rural MLAs have been among Government Agents' biggest allies. The following is an excerpt of the address given by the Hon. William Hartley, Minister of Public Works, to the citizens of Fort St. John on June 2, 1975 at the official opening ceremonies of the provincial government building and law courts:

> "We feel that the people, all of the people of British Columbia, are entitled to first- class service, and speaking of first-class service, one of the things that I learned before I was elected as an MLA-but certainly I have learned more of it as an MLA-is that if a person has a problem relative to the provincial government, well, the best place is to...make an appointment and sit down and chat with your Government Agent....
>
> "I have known in my own district of Nicola Valley-Merritt, that if there is a death in the family, either the husband or the wife has passed on, certainly that widow needs some help, and there is no better person to go to than your Government Agent.... In many cases, if it is a simple estate, that Government Agent can help you, with no fuss or furor, settle your estate.
>
> "Now this is something that has not been known too much in the past, wasn't advertised too widely, but we are proud of our Government Agents and of all our provincial public servants; they're dedicated, they work hard, they are more than security conscious...."

Moving On with the Times

Of course, enormous advancements in technology have taken place during the 150 years of Government Agents. Even over recent decades, huge changes have occurred.

Some of today's Government Agent staff remember sending messages on old teletype machines, receiving phone calls through a switchboard operator, and painting ink onto the roller of Gestetner machines to make multiple copies. There was even at

1930-1945
Government Agents' responsibilities include helping citizens with a form of social assistance, hospital insurance, and motor vehicle licensing.

one time something called an Address-O-Graph, a machine used for compiling the voters list. Staff also recall a time before the motto "share the air" when people wore perfume and customers could smoke in the office.

New cash registers arrived in every office in the Government Agent system in 1979, and staff attended training seminars to learn how to use them. The new CRISP system was a step up from the old registers and manual ledger books. Now Government Agents could capture transactions electronically and download them to Victoria. Weighing in at 80 pounds, the new registers ran on the first 51/4-inch floppy disks with a storage capacity of 360 kilobytes of information-tiny compared to today's average computer capacity of 870 gigabytes.

Red Alder Beauty

Never let it be said that fine art does not grace some Service BC Centres, for a magnificent carving sits high on the wall in centre court in the Vanderhoof centre.

In 1994, Peter Rodseth, a local artist, began to create a non-verbal expression of his passion for British Columbia: a massive, 3.2 metre-high, 12 metre-wide wooden sculpture. At the heart of the carving, surrounded by symbols for viewers to interpret as they see fit, sits a small gold star, representing Rodseth and, he says, all the citizens of this vast province.

A member of his family who was terminally ill at the time said she would not leave this life until the piece was finished. True to her word, she died four years later, just a few days after the artist finished his carving.

In September 1998, Vanderhoof resident Craig Hooper wrote the following poem about Rodseth's wooden carving:

The Alder Tree

There was an alder tree that stood
Where the stream ran through the wood,
And in its branches sparrows could
Sing forth their evening interlude,

In dark and dappled shade.

And when the east wind storms were straining,
Against its scattered leaves remaining,
The grey November clouds came raining,

To lash the alder glade.

The tree stood proud in summer light,
In moon bright snow on Winter's night,
Within its boughs birds sought respite,
And then burst forth in sudden flight.

And at its base the wild deer laid.

Woodcutters came one day and found,
Its towering grace and then the sound
Of saws, they made the woods resound.
And into boards the tree was made.

A woodcarver bought and took them home,
And in his mind there burned a poem,
That he would carve in wood alone,
To make his Valley's wonders known.

And so his plans were made.

His forebears carved Norwegian wood,
With hand and eye and steel they could,
Make things of beauty, pure and good,

That time's passage could not fade.

The valley, the river, the people, the land,
Would spring to life beneath Peter's hand,
Chisel and skew at this command,
In forms that all could understand.

A song that must be played.

The task took on a daunting tone,
A muttered word, a sigh, a groan,
The carver felt a weight like stone.

But the course he stayed.

The fireweed blooms and dies,
Geese circle where the river sighs,
The carver hears the haunting cries,
and so another year slips by,

1930s

Gold commissioner duties are extended. They have, since 1858, been charged with the responsibility of administering the estates of free miners who died without heirs or administrators. This authority is extended at this time to include non-free miners, by making many Government Agents official administrators.

His monument unmade.

The fragrant shavings spiral forth,
Returning geese come from the North,
The carver's light it shines before us,

A light that will not fade

The alder is now raised on high,
In dappled light to please the eye,
Of village folk and passers-by,
And once again the eagle flies.

Above the alder wood.

THE PREMIER GIVES THE NOD

Legislation exists to govern every British Columbia department except for one: Government Agents. Throughout much of its history this branch has had no formal legislation for the work it does. Even today, as Service BC Centres, it exists solely to carry out the programs of other branches; almost every government program has at some point in time flowed through its offices.

Government Agents conference, Victoria, B.C., November 8 and 9, 1973.

On four occasions—in 1965, 1973, 1976, and 1987—the premier or a minister acting on the premier's and cabinet's behalf has "petitioned agents to take full advantage of their unique place in district administration."

The premier and ministers were speakers at a conference of Government Agents in the 1970s and personally delivered the message.

1930s
During the years of the Great Depression, several Government Agent offices are reduced to sub-offices.

MANY EXAMPLES EXIST OF GOVERNMENT AGENTS' DEDICATION to their job and the personal imprint they put on their portfolios. Here are just a few.

THE GOVERNMENT OF
THE PROVINCE OF BRITISH COLUMBIA

NOTICE.

The attention of the officials and staff of all Government Agencies is called to the nature of the oath taken on entering the Civil Service :—

"I, _____, do swear that I will faithfully and honestly, to the utmost of my ability, perform all the duties which devolve upon me as_____ in the employment of the Executive Government of the Province of British Columbia, and that I will not disclose or make known any matter or thing which comes to my knowledge by reason of my employment therein, except in so far as my official duty requires me to disclose, make known, report upon, or take official action regarding the same, or except in so far as I may be duly authorized to disclose or make known the same."

All Civil Servants are strictly enjoined that no business matters coming under their notice are to be discussed except with authorized officials of the Department, and no information as to Agency business or matters affecting the staff are to be given to any one whatever, except to those legally entitled to the same.

In connection with the serious nature of a breach of these regulations, attention is called to the following extract of section 86 of the "Criminal Code of Canada" :—

"Every one who by means of his holding or having held an office under His Majesty has lawfully or unlawfully either obtained possession of or control over any document, sketch, plan, or model, or acquired any information, and at any time, corruptly or contrary to his official duty, communicates or attempts to communicate such document, sketch, plan, model, or information to any person to whom the same ought not, in the interests of the State, or otherwise in the public interests, to be then communicated, is guilty of an indictable offence, and liable :—

"(a.) If the communication was made or attempted to be made to a foreign State, to imprisonment for life ; and

"(b.) In any other case, to imprisonment for one year, or to a fine not exceeding $100, or to both imprisonment and fine."

BY ORDER,

Minister of Finance.

This Notice must be kept posted WITHIN all Government Agencies, and shall be constantly under the observation of members of the Staff.

Alice Pallard's signature, second from the bottom, on her oath of employment, dated August 1952. Her last name was Oakes at the time.

STILL GOING STRONG

As a marriage commissioner in Golden since 1982, Alice Pallard has performed about 800 marriages, some in her own home, some at the top of Kicking Horse Mountain Resort, and some in grassy fields and by the rivers that run through town. She performed the very first wedding on the Eagle Eye Express Gondola at Kicking Horse Mountain Resort.

Surely Pallard is one of the most innovative marriage commissioners in British Columbia. One couple did not have wedding rings, so she fashioned two of them out of paper clips.

After another ceremony, when the moment came for photographs of the bride and groom, the bride did not want her picture taken. What to do? Pallard stepped in, of course, and her photo was taken alongside the groom.

Another couple wanted to be married on a glacier at 2:00 in the afternoon. When that time arrived and a safe landing place had not been found, Pallard performed the ceremony while they circled the glacier. The pilot and his wife acted as witnesses.

Two years ago, Pallard was game enough to ride on the back of a snowmobile for half an hour to arrive at a wedding location. Perhaps not surprisingly, she does not recall that marriage with particular fondness.

She performed a wedding one day at Emerald Lake Lodge, outside of Field, and then raced home just in time to be with her dying mother. The dedicated commissioner drove back to Field the very next morning to perform another wedding.

Perhaps the most auspicious ceremony of all occurred when she married two people on top of Golden's local landmark, Mount 7, on the seventh day of the seventh month at 7:00 p.m. in 2007.

Pallard continues to perform marriage ceremonies-at the age of 86!

BOUNDARY'S FIRST GOVERNMENT AGENT

The same Constable William McMynn that took part in the Gold Brick Robbery later became Boundary's first Government Agent. His dedication to his government posts created a legacy in the region; the McMynn family is prominent in the area to this day.

Born on March 14, 1864 near Kirkcudbright, Scotland, McMynn came to Canada as a teenager and fell in love with the Boundary region. After a brief return to his native country, he returned with his older brother, Thomas, and settled in the Kettle Valley. Thomas was killed in 1892 in a horseback riding incident, and McMynn's two younger brothers, James and Edward, eventually joined him in Canada. In the meantime, McMynn managed several properties he and Thomas had very successfully farmed, one of which was McMynn Meadows, a few kilometres southwest of Camp McKinney, near where the famous Gold Brick Robbery took place. He also owned a mineral claim at Camp McKinney.

McMynn became a member of the provincial police on July 1, 1892, and in December of that year was appointed a district recorder of mines for the newly created mining division for Boundary. He went on to more government posts, including notary public and justice of the peace for the Yale electoral district in 1893, responsible for public works (without extra pay), and registrar of the county court in Midway in 1894.

After the Gold Brick Robbery, McMynn's police work increased considerably, and by 1897, he was chief constable.

In May 1900, he moved with his family to Greenwood and became the region's first Government Agent. McMynn added warden of Oakalla Prison Farm to his formidable list of job titles in 1912, and superintendent of the B.C. provincial police in 1918.

He died in his sleep in August 1929 at the Qualicum Beach Hotel while on holiday there with his wife and is buried in the Royal Oak Cemetery in Victoria. His was a long and legendary career.

A POLITICAL SLANT

Government Agents sometimes ventured into politics. At one point they held two-thirds of the legislative council for the mainland portion of the Colony of British Columbia.

One such agent was Andrew Charles Elliott, who in 1865 was a council member while at the same time he retained his position as magistrate. Two years later he became high sheriff for the Colony of British Columbia and then, in 1875, an MLA in the new Province of British Columbia. From 1876 to 1879 he served as British Columbia's fourth premier.

But not everyone was happy that a magistrate had been appointed to political posts, especially when Elliott took a different road and, on more than one occasion, clashed with New Westminster and, later, Victoria. His problem-solving solutions were apparently unique.

Colonel Moody, for example, did not approve of Elliott having the authority to select sites for towns, reserves for military purposes, or determine roadways, all powers held by Government Agents at that time. Moody felt that such decisions should be sanctioned by him alone, and he went as far as writing a letter to Governor James Douglas imploring him to reconsider.

A plaque in Elliott's honour sits today in the Lillooet Service BC Centre. It designates Elliott as "Prime Minister of British Columbia," a title that was sometimes given then to premiers or presidents of the executive council. It reads:

THE HONOURABLE ANDREW C. ELLIOTT
PRIME MINISTER OF BRITISH COLUMBIA

1876-1879

First County Court Judge for Yale and Hope, appointed by Sir James Douglas, Governor January 10th, 1860

Barrister of Inner Temple who became Government Agent at Lillooet in 1859

First County Court Judge named on the Mainland of British Columbia and his jurisdiction included all British territory on the Mainland of the Colony

Andrew Charles Elliott, British Columbia's fourth premier.

1942
Appointment of Jessie Foster of Williams Lake, the first woman Government Agent.

An Active Member of the Community

Wayne Hakanson served as Trail's Government Agent from August 2000 to July 2007. However, during his tenure he did so much more. He was an active member of the community and participated in numerous committees, including the Rotary Club, treasurer and vice-president of the chamber of commerce, treasurer of the Columbia Mountain Open Network (CMON), member and director of the Trail Festival Society, and a founding member of the Trail Arts Centre.

The Trail chamber of commerce's 1994 report mentioned Hakanson's work with CMON and a 2003 premier's Technology Council Pilot Project as a major accomplishment. The pilot project joined with School District No. 20 to connect all of the provincial government offices, schools, and colleges in the school district to a fibre optic network. One of the project's main objectives was to connect the three local high schools to broadband and provide the students with access to more courses and more teachers via the high-speed network.

Hakanson also arranged for a Columbia River sign to be posted on the Trail bridge. The chamber had been requesting a sign there for 10 years, but he was the one who made it happen. Within weeks of his taking on the assignment, a sign was posted on the bridge.

Mistaken Identity

George Christie Tunstall arrived in British Columbia as one of the Overlanders of 1862, a party of would-be prospectors and miners who travelled from Ontario to join the Cariboo gold rush. He eventually became gold commissioner and Government Agent, first of Granite City and then of Revelstoke. (His son, G.C. Tunstall Jr., was purser on the sternwheeler S.S. Lytton, one of the early vessels on the Arrow Lakes.)

Tunstall's last posting was as Government Agent in Kamloops, which is where he attained local fame. He was a big man, and contemporary accounts of him suggest that he had a fiery temper, which may explain how he got into trouble on at least one occasion.

A prisoner had escaped from the Kamloops jail. Strolling through town one day, Tunstall encountered a man who fitted the general description of the escaped prisoner and who could not give a satisfactory account of himself-because he spoke no English. Still, he looked like the right man, and that was enough for Tunstall, who seized him by the scruff of the neck and the seat of his pants and bundled him off to the lock-up.

Later someone with first-hand knowledge of the escapee took a look at Tunstall's captive and said, "Tunstall, you've got the wrong man!" Chastened, Tunstall released his prisoner, apologized, shook his hand, and gave him five dollars out of his own pocket. It is not known what the captive thought of all of this, but he did leave Kamloops soon after his release.

Taking Delivery

Right from the beginning, the northern town of Stewart has enjoyed the benefits of having popular and public-spirited Government Agents. John Conway was always in the fore of hospital, lodge, dance, and concert committees between 1910 and 1920. His successor, John P. Scarlett, was more reserved, but always ready to give a helping hand. He was active on the hospital board and always enjoyed playing his cello in the orchestra.

Gordon Swan was the last Government Agent to actually live in the Stewart court-house, which served as the Government Agent office. During his time in Stewart, Swan was the fire chief, local assistant to the fire commissioner, area co-ordinator for the provincial emergency program, and treasurer and president of the Stewart/Hyder international chamber of commerce. He also spent a year collecting much of the information that comprises this book.

Probably the most colourful agent in Stewart was Harry W. Dodd, who was transferred to Stewart in 1932 after 24 years in Telegraph Creek. He had been posted to Telegraph Creek in 1908 and was appointed a provincial police constable the following year. In 1923, he was transferred from the force to become, in turn, mining recorder, gold commissioner, Government Agent, judge, and, probably his

The courthouse in Stewart has always been (and still is) the Government Agent office.

Mid-1940s
Following World War II, Government Agents become involved in the calculation and collection of school taxes from 60 newly established school districts.

most illustrious position, government liquor vendor. From September 1921 to July 1929, he held all five positions at the same time.

One fall, in Stewart, Dodd provided a service of a different nature. Two big game hunters from New York sought to obtain their hunting permits, only to be informed that the Government Agent was busy-attending to the delivery of a baby. The hunters then identified themselves as doctors and asked to be directed to the expectant mother. Upon their arrival, they found mother and baby doing well, thanks to Dodd's tender care. The astounded doctors later sent him a set of medical reference books to help him with his "extra line of endeavour."

"Big Jack" Kirkup

People called John Kirkup "Big Jack" for good reason. He was big-well over 200 pounds and maybe closer to 300-strong and tough as they came, with a rough-and-tumble style of governing. There was federal law, there was provincial law, and there was Big Jack Kirkup's law. If there was trouble in one of the saloons, he simply banged a couple of heads together. Hollywood legend has it that John Wayne fashioned himself after Kirkup's unique use of his gun: rather than shooting someone, he just belted them across the face with it.

After a stint as constable in Yale, Kirkup moved to Revelstoke and became Government Agent in 1892 or 1893. One day he discovered a squatter had built his shack by a stream that served as a source of drinking water. When Kirkup was unable to convince the squatter to move the structure, he simply pushed it over-with the squatter still in it.

This did nothing to endear him to the citizens of Revelstoke, who sent a petition to the Attorney General: "We, the undersigned, business men of Revelstoke, do beg you will favourably consider the advisability of removing the Government Agent to a more congenial sphere.... We do not want to make any personal charges although we can do so, but we desire his quiet removal to some other post where he can not damage our town and district...."

Kirkup was transferred to Rossland as Government Agent in 1896.

He possessed tenacity. He once pursued a wanted criminal south over the border, followed him across eight states, and eventually caught the fugitive in Chicago. The man was brought back to British Columbia where he was tried and hanged.

Kirkup was transferred to Alberni in 1912 as Government Agent and served there for three years before moving to Nanaimo on July 1, 1915. He died from diabetes on

November 16, 1916 and is buried in the Nanaimo cemetery. Mount Kirkup, near Rossland, bears his name, as well as Kirkup Creek, near Revelstoke.

Constable Big Jack Kirkup.

1947
Government Agents are used for the conversion and continued maintenance of the permanent voters list.

The Government Agent office in Barkerville becomes the largest mining office in British Columbia.

THE LOVELY KASLO COURTHOUSE

The first Government Agent office in Kaslo was located at 413 B Avenue, but moved to its present location in the town's lovely, historic courthouse, with its gracefully curved, exterior double staircase. The building was erected during 1911 to 1912 at 416 A Avenue for $42,000.

The mining recorder and assessor, the registrar, a constable (probably the provincial police), the timber inspector and fire warden, and of course the Government Agent shared the first floor, while the provincial and county court offices and the superintendent of roads occupied the second. Regular session of the provincial court ceased to be held here in the early 1980s. Today the courthouse provides space for the Service BC Centre, as well as Back on Track Productions, the Kaslo and District Community Forest Society, and the Kootenay Lake Archives.

Performing, as usual, many tasks, one early Government Agent acted as recording officer for the Kaslo cattle district in 1920. In 1937, he asked for, and received, "early retirement"-at the age of 68.

During the 1960s, due to the perceived threat of nuclear war, one of the rooms in the basement of the courthouse was converted to a fallout shelter. It is believed that this was intended for use by law enforcement and administrative agencies. Two prisoner lock-ups in the basement were in use until the mid-1960s. Now the old cells are being used for records.

The people who have worked on and in this building are as interesting as the building itself. For many years George Baker was the caretaker of the building and grounds. He is remembered for his lovely flower beds, particularly the dahlias. Andrew Jardine did some intriguing work on the building itself. In the original construction there were no electric light fixtures in the three large vaults. Jardine hand steeled through the vault walls to allow for wiring, declining to give a contract price. Instead he insisted on working for "miner's wages."

LATE 1940S - 1950S

Sources of revenue collected by Government Agents include amusement tax; court fees and fines; game licences and tags; hospital insurance premiums; land revenue; water licence fees; mining revenue; motor vehicle licences and fees and chauffeur licences; birth, death, and marriage certificates; trade licences; dog licences; social security and municipal aid tax; land taxes; as well as the sale of acts, survey posts, and poll tax.

Enjoying the Colourful Customers

CUSTOMERS COME IN ALL SHAPES AND SIZES. Sometimes the best part of a Government Agent's job is getting to know the people who come through the door.

IS YOUR WALLET DONE YET?

One Vernon Service BC Centre staff recalls a humorous incident:

"My customer, 'Jim,' came in to have his licence and care card replaced.
"'So what happened to your stuff?' I asked.
"'You don't really want to know, do you?' he replied.
"I said, 'Well, that's up to you,' and so Jim proceeded to tell me this story.
"He had gone on a holiday with his wife—well, first she was his wife, then she was his ex-wife-and had put his wallet in the microwave in their hotel room to hide it from thieves. Not realizing that the wallet had been stashed in the oven, she turned on the microwave to heat something up. His wallet was not only cooked-it caught on fire!
"After relaying this shocking tale, Jim produced his gnarled and twisted wallet from a little plastic bag. His driver's licence and other cards were totally melted into it, and his passport was half burnt. He said he was the laughing stock in the airports trying to get home with his cooked ID!"

IN MEMORY OF ART

Because of the sometimes personal nature of their work and because they regularly see the same customers in their office, friendships do occur between Government Agents and their customers. Squamish Service BC Centre staff recall one of their favourites:

"We first got to know Art over a year ago and were immediately enchanted by his sense of humour and zest for life. He visited our office to ask us questions about employment standards and then later to use our CATS terminal to apply for employment insurance and check the status of his application. He was in our office weekly, and every time we saw him he always had a smile and a friendly 'hello, ladies.'

"Early in 2007, we assisted him in applying for social services, after he was evicted from our local low-income housing complex when it was deemed inhabitable. Soon after moving from the complex, Art was diagnosed with liver cancer. He came to rely on us for the services we offered, like our assistance with applying for social services while in the hospital, answering questions and helping him with not only provincial government services, but community services as well. We tried to make sure he left our office feeling like he could come back at any time for whatever he needed. Even though Art's life was a roller coaster of ups and downs, we never saw his spirit waver.

"Christmas 2007 approached, and it seemed Art's spirit grew even brighter, despite the fact that his illness had progressed and become untreatable. As he moved through the motions of organizing the end of his life, his smile never dimmed, and he visited us frequently. He gave us a lovely poinsettia and a Christmas card that said we were his special angels and that he was looking forward to his 'next adventure.'

"He also thanked us, saying, 'I have never been treated with as much respect anywhere as I have been in your office.' This made us feel extremely special, and it was very clear to us that we had had an impact on Art that went beyond the customer service level to an emotional and personal level and that it meant a lot to him. It wasn't until he passed away that we realized that it meant a lot to us as well."

A Customer of a Different Order

Tax time always means extra work for Government Agents, but occasionally it also brings along requests far outside of the ordinary. Here is one recent story of how undaunted representatives stood up for a customer who lived in somewhat unusual circumstances.

An 80-year-old woman lived in the rural area of Fernie-with no electricity, no indoor plumbing, and no running water. Things were not about to change. This lack of utilities on the lady's taxes raised the suspicion of the Property Tax Branch in Victoria, and sure enough, one day the Government Agent at the time, Sharon Arola, received a phone call. Was it really true that there was no electricity, no plumbing, and no run-

Early 1960s
The Civil Service Commission requests Government Agents to act as field staffing co-ordinators.

ning water on the property? Arola confirmed that the woman had no plumbing, no running water, and no electricity at her house, so hence, she had no utilities.

Apparently no one in Victoria believed that an elderly person could still be living this way, so they actually sent an assessor to check out the property, who discovered, of course, that the agent had been right: the lady in question had no utilities on her property. The elderly woman continued to live there for many years afterward with no utilities, no plumbing, and no running water, a testament to the hardy pioneer spirit of the Elk Valley.

Ahoy, Matey

Early Government Agents were no strangers to making arrests, but in October 1898 one Vancouver Island agent was asked to capture "pirates."

Cumberland's Government Agent at the time, whose name was Anderson, got a telegram from Nanaimo to look out for three shipboard men who had robbed people in Englishman's River, Qualicum, and up and down the coast of Vancouver Island.

Anderson and his officer, Thompson, caught the three at the local wharf and, after a violent struggle, arrested them. The local newspaper, the Cumberland Semi-Weekly News, reported that "Government Agent Anderson was obliged to fell one of the robbers to the ground...in a hard fight."

Unfortunately, Anderson had been given incorrect information; he discovered afterward that there had in fact been four robbers, so the fourth one got away.

Privacy Goes Out the Window

Maple Ridge's Government Agent Cheryll Heroux says one of the most enjoyable and entertaining programs is mining. There was never a dull moment when she dealt with prospectors during her 17 years in the Princeton office, in a very busy mineral and placer area, including one who travelled in on his donkey.

Another old miner who had mineral claims in the Similkameen Mining Division for years came into their office:

> "He made regular trips to town and into the office to file work on his claims. He was very hard of hearing, so when he came into the office, we had to yell into his ear so he could hear us. We always heard him coming in, as he would yell, 'Heelllooo, Madam Gold Commissioner.'
>
> "He decided he should do something about his hearing, so he went

to the local Radio Shack and bought an amplifier box attached to two ear plugs. He didn't want to buy hearing aids, as they were too expensive. The plugs in his ears made things worse, as they blocked any sound going in and distorted his voice, so he yelled even louder. As we were talking to him, he would spend his time banging the amplifier on the counter trying to adjust it so he could hear us. The problem was that he often forgot to put in batteries, so we were basically yelling into the air. Our communication was always so loud that surely in the summer with the windows open, people passing by could have heard the entire transaction!"

THE COUGAR LADIES

The famous Cougar Ladies of the Sunshine Coast, Minnie and Bergie Solberg, were colourful customers of the Sechelt Government Agent office in the 1980s and 1990s. Living as trappers, hunters, guides, and loggers, both women boasted "hands like bear paws" and "skin thicker than sea lion leather." One friend remembers both for "a little too much spittin' on the floor."

Each year during hunting season Bergie Solberg came into the office to buy her hunting licence and at least one cougar tag. She would arrive wearing a crumpled cowboy hat, thick sweater, and baggy jeans, and carrying a jerry can to buy gas for the return trip to her boat-access-only cabin in a remote area of Sechelt Inlet. Since neither sister had phone or electricity at their cabins, they used the phone at the Sechelt office, often yelling into the receiver.

One year the local conservation officer, who shared his office with the Government Agent, tried to take Solberg's gun away for a violation. But she wrestled the officer to the floor of her cabin, saying there was "no way 'that man' was getting her gun."

Predeceased a year earlier by her sister, Solberg died in November 2002 at the age of 79 in her little cabin in the Sechelt Inlet.

TO THE ALTAR AND BACK

In 1979, Geraldine Schultz was working as Assistant Government Agent in Chetwynd, (there were no Deputy Government Agents in the smaller towns), and she was preparing to conduct her first marriage ceremony, which at that time had to be done in the office during normal business hours. The rest of the staff knew how excited Schultz was and made a big deal about her performing her very first wedding.

1970S
Government Agents become local representatives for the Criminal Injuries Program providing information, pamphlets, and application forms to those seeking assistance. They are also the first sellers of lottery tickets.

The bride and groom came, as planned, on a Friday afternoon, dressed in bridal gown and tuxedo, and Schultz conducted the entire event ceremony beautifully. On the following Monday, she came to work to find the groom sitting on the front steps of the office, still in his tuxedo and looking forlorn. To Schultz's surprise, he asked for an annulment. Apparently the bride had gone home to change after the ceremony- and had never come back. When the groom went home looking for her, he found his house had been cleaned out.

Schultz was able to have the marriage annulled: it had never been consummated.

Unusual Permits for Devil-Hunting

In the mid-1870s, there was a gold rush into the Cassiar district. Laketon, a settlement at the mouth of Dease Creek on the western shore of Dease Lake, was for many years the administrative centre of the district. J.L. Crimp was Laketon's gold commissioner, Government Agent, and constable. In 1876, he demonstrated a high degree of inventiveness and a sense of humour, both valuable assets in a frontier posting.

Sam Sing, a local miner, had two great passions in life: the pursuit of gold and the consumption of strong drink. Unfortunately, the gold he found seemed to wind up being converted into strong drink. When under its influence, Sing had visions of devils, demons, and other, more horrid things, which he felt were waiting to chase him through the streets of Laketon and out into the bush where, he feared, ferocious bears would devour him.

Sing took his problem to his Government Agent for resolution. Crimp and Sam discussed the matter and concluded that a special licence to shoot devils, demons, and nameless horrors would be the very thing. Crimp wrote out a special devil-hunting permit, signed it "Daniel O'Connell" and issued it to Sing, who went away overjoyed. He was so overjoyed, in fact, that he got howling drunk. That evening, the good people of Laketon had to dive for cover, because Sam stood in the middle of the street, revolver in one hand, devil-hunting permit in the other, blazing away at things only he could see.

1973
Government Agents assist the government, landlords, and tenants in resolving residential tenancy matters.

⊷ Going the Extra Mile ⊶

N<small>O MATTER WHAT THE REQUEST</small>, G<small>OVERNMENT</small> A<small>GENTS</small> always respond to the best of their ability. And sometimes they go that extra mile.

S<small>AVING THE</small> D<small>AY</small>

One morning in June 2007, five disabled adults and a care worker arrived at a sporting goods shop in Vancouver to purchase fishing licences. However, only one of them had previously purchased the special licence for those with disabilities allowing them to fish for a nominal $1 fee. The other four needed to fill out applications and have them certified. Unfortunately, the vendor could not approve the applications right there on the spot because they had not been signed off by each person's health care provider. But the outing had been arranged, the van was waiting, and they wanted to go fishing.

Because the vendor had been selling fishing licences for more than 50 years, he knew who to call for a solution: the Sechelt Service BC Centre.

Realizing the urgency of the situation, one Sechelt Service BC Centre staff quickly suggested that if the caregiver accompanying the adults would commit to getting the special applications completed after the fact, then the vendor could in fact sell them the discounted licences that morning. In the end, everyone was able to buy their licences and enjoy their day of fishing.

When the completed documents arrived, they were accompanied by a personal note: "At last we are able to send you the signed applications. I would like to thank you again for your kind service.... [We] wish you all the best!" This staff member found a way to get the job done and keep the customer satisfied.

N<small>OT IN THE</small> J<small>OB</small> D<small>ESCRIPTION</small>

Moving house? It's not in the Government Agent job description, but.... In 1972, Fort Nelson's Government Agent, Norm Schultz, was assigned the task of organizing, preparing, and executing two household moves for the new public health nurse and the weigh scale supervisor. Each was to move into their own trailer.

Schultz was happy to oversee this assignment, until he discovered that construction workers had placed wooden two-by-fours beneath the trailers rather than the concrete pillars required by town law. When he advised the workers about this, they told him to do it himself, and that is exactly what this Government Agent did.

Schultz not only arranged for the Ministry of Forests to clear the land and for the Department of Highways to clear and level it, he also had the trailers relocated and mounted in the proper manner. But he did not stop there. He installed flooring, carpet, and curtains, and furnished the trailers right down to the knives and forks in the kitchen drawers. Only one item was missing when the new residents moved in: Victoria kept sending toilet seats, but not the toilets.

IN THE TUB

Invermere Service BC Centre staff played an important role in a near-miss wedding:

"Our office in Invermere issued a marriage licence to a young couple from Calgary, Alberta. Two weeks later I received a call from a lady in Cochrane, Alberta, two and a half hours away. She said she had found a tub on the side of the highway that contained a marriage licence, wedding rings, and gifts for a wedding party. She had obtained our office number through directory assistance and was asking us what she should do.

"I requested that she send the tub to our location, as I expected the couple would show up for a replacement licence once they discovered the problem. I asked the caller for the names on the marriage licence and immediately began calling everyone in the area with the same last names.

"Just as I was losing hope, on the last call I connected with the mother of the groom. The couple had arrived at her home the day before. They had not yet unloaded their vehicle and therefore were not aware the tub was missing. I gave her the number of the lady who had found the tub, and arrangements were made to courier it to Invermere.

"The wedding was held successfully the following Saturday."

ALL IN A DAY'S WORK

No Government Agent expects to be trapping wildlife in the course of their working day. But sometimes that is just what happens.

The phone rang in the Kelowna office one day. Even though it was past closing time, the Government Agent answered the phone expecting to hear a shopping list

1973-1983
Government Agents are used by the Insurance Corporation of British Columbia as insurance brokers. Today only two offices still administer this program: Atlin and Dease Lake. However, many more offices are still heavily involved in all aspects of the driver's licensing function.

from his wife. Instead it was a member of the public complaining that a pheasant had invaded a Rutland home. The agent took up the challenge.

He called the Fish and Wildlife Branch, but no answer. He considered the responsibilities under the Health Act and the Residential Tenancy Act, but decided he could not pass the buck. Then he had an idea. He rushed down to the local, friendly sporting goods store and borrowed, for undisclosed purposes, the largest fishing net he could find. So armed, he raced off to the complainant's house.

The Government Agent missed the pheasant on the first pass with the net and pursued the feathered fugitive around the living room floor in wild circles, until he almost forgot who was chasing whom. At last he trapped the frightened ring neck, stopping only to look at the wreckage noting extensive damage to glassware and the splattering of a certain substance upon the furniture. He released the unharmed bird to its natural wildlife habitat-far from the home of the complainant.

He returned the fishing net to the sporting goods store without commenting on the "heroic" purpose for which it had been used. He made a mental note to record the overtime with a plea for inclusion in a pre-retirement leave for special circumstances.

The next day a detailed description of the wild chase appeared in the Daily Courier.

Greater than the Sum of their Parts

Government Agents do not always get to help members of the public in such a dramatic way; most of the time their job requires them to help citizens with the details of their day-to-day lives. Yet those details can have a significant impact on a person's life. Obtaining a driver's licence in a remote community, for example, gives a person mobility. In other words, Government Agents' jobs are greater than the sum of their parts.

J.R. Brown was one such Government Agent at the turn of the 20th century whose work added much to the districts in which he lived. He came to Vernon, B.C., from Scotland in 1893, at the age of 39, after farming sheep in New Zealand and ranching on the Canadian prairies.

Brown moved with his family to Penticton and became a police constable. There he began a career in the civil service that would span more than 30 years and take him to Osoyoos as mining recorder and Fairview in a multitude of agency positions, including stipendiary magistrate. For a while he even ran the Fairview post office. The house that Brown built in 1897 still stands on its original site in town.

He was a well-respected man, admired and held in high esteem by the local First Nations, early mining folk, and settlers. As a provincial government employee he played an important role in the maintenance of law and order in the Okanagan Valley and especially in Fairview.

Noel Stirling Austin Arnold-Wallinger was another such hard-working Government Agent. He immigrated from England to Calgary, Alberta in 1885 and

The office and residence of J.R. Brown, tireless government employee for more than 30 years.

moved to Golden, B.C., and then Fort Steele a year later, where he began his life-long career in public service. He worked on the railway for the B.C. government and prospected as a free miner and trapped for almost a decade before returning to England briefly to marry.

In 1895, Arnold-Wallinger and his new wife moved to the Kootenays, and he became a mining broker. In 1905, he accepted a promotion to clerk in the Government Agent office in Cranbrook as a means to educate his growing family of seven children and five years later was appointed mining recorder in Fort Steele. He rose to Government Agent and gold commissioner in Cranbrook in 1913, performing those functions until 1922, when he began a six-year career in the B.C. legislature as an MLA for the Cranbook area. Arnold-Wallinger resumed his post as Government Agent in Cranbrook in 1928 and retired in 1932.

LIKE SO MANY OTHERS

Elon Ezra Chipman was typical of all conscientious Government Agents all over British Columbia who work to a high standard day after day and give their very best to the job.

1975
The end of Government Agent involvement with courts due to government restructuring, although some remote offices still have some involvement on the court's behalf.

Chipman was born in Ontario on March 9, 1846. He came to government circuitously after experimenting with several professions, including teaching school for six years, journalism and publishing a newspaper for one year, and the mercantile business. But in 1880 he discovered prospecting and for the next 10 years mined all over Colorado, Idaho, Utah, and Montana and then, finally the Rocky Mountains in British Columbia. Chipman settled in Kaslo, B.C., where he became one of its most valued citizens.

He resumed his mining operations there until 1896. Modest and hard-working, his skills could not help but be noticed by the government, who offered him a position as city clerk and then, because of his excellent job performance over the next four and a half years, promoted him to police magistrate. By 1900, he was stipendiary magistrate, Government Agent, and gold commissioner for the Slocan district, covering both Kaslo and Slocan. Chipman held all of these positions for 13 years.

He was noted for being farsighted and capable in the public service. Few if any men were better known in the community and the surrounding area of the time than Chipman. Like so many other Government Agents before and after, he contributed much to the province of British Columbia.

One Way to Keep an Account Up To Date

Government Agents have always provided high-level service to the public, but often a little extra collaboration, hard work, and perseverance with customers creates unexpected success.

The public often views collection activity, for example, somewhat negatively, when in fact the agent's goal is to help the taxpayer be successful. One event in Nanaimo is a case in point.

A customer was seriously delinquent on property taxes and unable to pay, and the subsequent penalty and interest had continued to accumulate, thereby increasing the overdue taxes every month. People sometimes do not realize that a home owner grant can be claimed even though taxes cannot be paid; this customer thought the total amount of overdue tax had to be paid and did not realize that small amounts can be paid any time.

Government Agent staff worked with the taxpayer to claim late home owner grants and establish a payment schedule to catch up the delinquent taxes, starting out with a very small amount and gradually increasing to larger payments. Although property taxes can be prepaid, there was no method in place to provide for monthly prepayment. So the agency staff set up a local prepaid account into which the customer could deposit a small monthly amount.

The customer came into the office every month to pay the agreed-upon amount of tax until the account was up to date. This proved so successful that they wanted to continue paying monthly-even after the taxes were no longer delinquent.

Every month for the past seven or eight years this customer has visited the office to make payments. The tax account was never delinquent again.

ROOTS

One day a young woman came into the Campbell River Service BC Centre with an odd request: she wanted help finding the house her mother had been born in and in which she herself had lived until the age of three. However, because she was due to return home to Germany in just a few hours, there was very little time.

The staff were eager to help but had little to go on. Judith provided her mother's name and birth date and her deceased grandmother's name, Margaret. After some further conversation with Judith, staff saw in her eyes the deep desire to find a connection with her mother and grandmother. They set to work.

They started by contacting the local municipal office, but it had no residency records that would shed light. They then called the local assessment office, which did not have records that went back that far. The Government Agent then contacted the Regional Director of Vital Statistics to see if information could be found quickly that would show Judith's grandparents' address. This too ended up being a dead end, as all Vital Statistics could offer was for Judith to try a genealogy search. At this point staff phoned the seniors in the community to see if anyone could remember "Grandma Margaret."

Time was running short, and many, many calls were made with no success. Staff noticed the disappointment on Judith's face. They were down to the last two names of people who might have been able to help. Just as they asked her for future contact information, a woman named Joyce called and said that not only had she known Margaret, but she had worked for Margaret's husband back in the early 1950s.

Joyce rushed down to the office to meet with Judith, but the good news went even further: Joyce knew someone in town named Dolly, who had known Judith's grandmother and mother very well. As Judith and Joyce talked, staff tried to contact Dolly, but she was not home, and Judith had to go. Tears flowed as Joyce and Judith hugged and said goodbye. Unfortunately, Joyce did not know the location of the house Judith was looking for, but felt sure Dolly would. Numbers were exchanged so that photos of the house could be sent via email, and Judith left Campbell River with a happy heart.

Two days later staff received a call from Joyce, who informed them that she had arranged for Dolly to contact Judith by phone. Dolly not only knew the house but also believed she had photos of Judith's mother and grandmother, which she would send to Judith. Tears were shed during that phone call as well, this time by delighted staff.

The representatives could have said there was nothing more they could do for Judith when their first attempts with government agencies failed. They were all busy that day. But they chose to go the extra mile and were glad they did. As always, they put themselves in the customer's position and treated her the way they would have liked to be treated themselves.

1977
The first attempt is made to draft a Government Agent job description.

Government Agents assist the ombudsman in their work on request.

Telling a Good Story

GOVERNMENT AGENTS TELL IT BEST, IN THEIR OWN WORDS.

ONE WAY TO GET A DRIVER'S LICENCE

Today there is a graduated driver's licensing program before one takes to the road. Things were a little different in Burns Lake in the 1950s, when it appears it was much easier to get a licence.

The Government Agent office had recently opened, and Aubrey Fisher was the first agent in Burns Lake. Jean Patterson recalls how she got her driver's licence there:

> "I was 21 or so years old at that time, and my husband Archie and I drove in from Colleymount in our little Jeep. Archie took me to see the district police officer/wildlife officer, Bill Richmond, for a driver's test. Bill was busy at the time and did not have time to administer the test.
>
> "He asked Archie whether I could drive. Archie, of course, said yes and that I had been practising on the farm. Bill then told Archie to take me to the Government Agent's office and tell Aubrey Fisher, the Government Agent, to issue me a driver's licence.
>
> "And that's how I got my driver's licence in 1950. I drove with that licence for two years, and I didn't need to take an exam nor a driver's test in a vehicle."

QUEEN CHARLOTTE REFLECTIONS

Monica Jones, Government Agent in the Queen Charlotte Islands/Haida Gwaii, describes her introduction to the branch:

> "I first heard of Government Agents during a trip to the Queen Charlottes. Driving down the main road, my attention was caught by the large Government Agent sign on a nondescript building. What on earth kind of office was this? It conjured up thoughts of James Bond and secret government spy work. Why would they advertise such a clandestine place on the side of a building, and why did a tiny place like

Queen Charlotte need such a presence?

"I actually set foot into that office a couple of years later, a brand new B.C. resident fresh off the ferry, ready to start my new life in Queen Charlotte. In a small, isolated community like Queen Charlotte, the Service BC Centre is a prominent face of government and often the first stop for residents and visitors looking for a mind-boggling assortment of information. It was time to take care of all the humdrum details like obtaining a driver's licence. (So that's what a Government Agent did!) I did not have high hopes about a tiny government office in such a remote and isolated place. Would they know what to do with an out-of-country driver's licence? Had they ever seen one, even?

"Imagine my surprise when a customer service representative greeted me with a huge smile. Welcome! Transfer a U.S. driver's licence to B.C.? No problem! Did I need any other newcomer information? Could she help me set up my B.C. medical coverage? Would I like to have a sneak peek at my driver's licence photo? If I didn't like it, she'd take another!

"I left the office, shaking my head in amazement. Every subsequent visit to the office reaffirmed the positive experience I'd had. Documents were efficiently notarized. What I thought would be a long wait in line one day turned out to be no more than a few minutes, thanks to the way that staff tactfully and expertly handled their customers, whom they obviously knew well. Whenever I called the office with questions, either a live person answered the phone or a phone message was promptly returned. Referrals to other offices were cheerfully provided when I needed information."

THE CORONER, THE DECEASED, AND THE PICKUP TRUCK

From the 1860s to the 1980s, and possibly as late as the 1990s in a few remote locations in British Columbia, the job of medical examiner fell to Government Agents. Training was sometimes a little less than perhaps one would have wished, as can be seen by this story of a young Lorne Wilson providing relief for Phil Welock in the summer of 1983:

"In August 1983, I travelled to Atlin to substitute for the Government Agent, Phil Welock. He graciously left me his living quarters, which

1978
Government Agents assist in registering and regulating the movement of manufactured homes.

1987
Agents act as strike vote observers.

was half of the office building, his boat, and even his springer spaniel, Sadie, who had an unfortunate obsession of rolling in fresh horse manure given the opportunity. My wife, Wendy, loved that.

"One Sunday we returned from fishing to find the town nurse on our doorstep. She advised that a miner had died a few days earlier in his cabin. I thought that perhaps she was looking for a burial permit as Government Agents were district registrars for Vital Statistics. She advised me, however, that the Government Agent was the coroner, and I needed to examine the corpse. I was a trifle surprised by this (!) and sought advice from the regional coroner, Bob Graham.

"As the local RCMP officer and I approached the cabin, it was indeed obvious by the odour that a death had occurred. We placed the corpse in a body bag and carried it to a pickup truck owned by the local hotel proprietor for transport to Whitehorse for the autopsy. I later learned that the hotel proprietor was anxious to help as the Province paid $50 for loading, which he didn't do, and $400 for transport to Whitehorse. This was a significant sum in those years. I told Wendy that I would have strapped the miner to the seat of our car and conversed with him all the way to Whitehorse had I known that.

"It must have been a rather difficult autopsy after the corpse had bounced around on 60 miles of gravel road in the back of a pickup on its way to Whitehorse.

It's another example of why our organization is an interesting place to work."

Blowing Off the Dust

Staff in the Fernie Service BC Centre discovered some interesting history:

"We found some dusty old ledger books in our archives. The penmanship in these ledgers is amazing with beautiful, old-style, swirly, embellished handwriting obviously done with an old-fashioned pen dipped in ink. These ledgers reveal interesting entries that show what the Fernie Government Agent did in the year 1912. For instance, in July of that year, the agent issued 55 cheques totalling $34,923.87.

"The Provincial Secretary gave out vouchers and financial assistance for such things as:

> $25.00 to someone to bury another person who had been destitute
> $20.00 to a doctor for an Elko typhoid epidemic
> $4.00 for a load of wood for a destitute woman
> $5.00 to a doctor for examining someone for insanity
> $300.00 for fare to Austria for a woman and four children
> $16.15 for goods to a drug company for someone who was quarantined.

"Paid on behalf of the Attorney General were

> $8.95 for transportation of a constable and prisoners
> $55.00 to the City of Fernie for the keep of prisoners.

"The Minister of Finance paid for things like

> $18.00 for Government Agent expenses
> $3.00 for the destruction of wolves, panthers, and coyotes
> $301.00 per month for civil government salaries for the Fernie agency
> $150.00 per month for the Inspector of Mines' salary
> $2.00 for bounty on one big-horned owl
> $6.00 for the destruction of a golden eagle
> $8.50 for mine rescue in Fernie.

"On behalf of Public Works a cheque for $3.25 was issued for shoeing the Road Superintendent's horse."

A Guy Like You in a Job Like This

Government Agent Peter Lee recalls his early days in the Squamish office:

"In the summer of 1980, the Government Agent's branch was in expansion mode, opening new offices in Sechelt, Squamish, Chetwynd, McKenzie, Valemount, and Sparwood. All six Government Agent positions were offered under one competition, with the most highly qualified candidate being offered their first choice of the six locations.

"As a young 25-year-old management trainee working out of the

1988
First access centre opens in Fort St. John co-locating with other ministries.

Late 1980s
Agents sell B.C. Savings Bonds.

Prince Rupert agency, I was lucky enough to be interviewed and, although I didn't come in first in the competition, I was very fortunate to be offered the position of Government Agent at Squamish.

"It took a tremendous amount of work to get the new office up and running with recruiting and training new staff, transferring program delivery responsibilities from other community service providers to include with the agency portfolio, and marketing the new office in the service area. We all thoroughly enjoyed the effort, and we were very proud of the new office.

"Soon after the office opened, I was very excited to have the opportunity of a visit to our office by Chief Leo of the Mount Currie Band and gave him a tour of the operation. Chief Leo listened intently as I showed him around and explained the range of services provided by the Government Agent's branch. He appeared to be quite impressed. At the door, as he was about to leave the office, I asked him if he had any further questions. He turned to me and said, 'Only one.... How does a guy like you get a job like this?'"

The Hijackers

Government services were provided in the Queen Charlotte Islands/Haida Gwaii from 1873 to 1874, then from 1912 to the present day, although not always from an office on the island. Since the early 1970s, however, there has been a permanent Government Agent office in the Charlottes-once in the old hospital. The office moved into its fourth and current location in 1993, which contains a courtroom that is used once a month when Prince Rupert court staff come over to the island to hold court.

One local island, as well as a mountain near Golden, is named after the 1912 Queen Charlotte Government Agent, E.M. Sandilands.

Audrey Hoy, Customer Service Representative in Prince Rupert, has fond memories of travelling to Queen Charlotte to assist the Government Agent office. One trip was a little precarious though.

She and two other passengers were stranded at Anna Lake on a return flight from Queen Charlotte because the plane she was on showed a drop in oil pressure. The pilot assured them that the nearby logging camp would probably put them up if he did not return by nightfall and then took off.

As the three "castaways" were contemplating the rather unpleasant turn of events, another plane landed to unload supplies and they decided it was now or never, marched up to the new plane and boldly loaded their luggage. The pilot realized what was happening and protested vehemently, but they ignored him, climbed aboard and strapped themselves in. "You are taking us back to Sandspit!" they announced. After a flurry of radio communication, the pilot took his "hijackers" back to Sandspit, where they transferred to another floatplane and continued on to Prince Rupert.

LEARNING THE ROPES

Campbell River's Government Agent, Jeff MacKenzie, says that recording mining claims is one of his favourite tasks. But it was not always that way:

> "It was November of 1982. I had been a Management Trainee in the Nanaimo Government Agent office for six months when the call came for my first relief mission into Ucluelet. Up until this time, the focus of my training had been in the ICBC Insurance and Vital Statistics programs. Although new, I felt confident I could handle this duty. To be sure, I phoned the then Government Agent Gerri Taron to ask her a few questions about what to expect. She told me not to worry, as the late fall and winter months were quiet times, and the needs of the local populace centred on making simple payments to B.C. Medical and asking general questions.
>
> "'Great, but what about mining?' I asked, as I had no training in that area yet. Taron assured me that Ucluelet and Tofino had only one free-miner, and he never attended the office during the fall and winter. Excellent!
>
> "I arrived at work early the following Monday morning, so I could acquaint myself with the office. Taron had left by then, so I was working on my own. Promptly at 8:30 a.m., I opened the office doors and went back to my desk to sit down. At 8:32 a.m., a gentleman walked into the office with maps, papers, and assorted drawing gadgets.
>
> "'How can I help you?' I asked.
>
> "'I would like to record some mining claims,' he replied. Well, imagine my face when he said that.
>
> "Back then, the recording of claims and anything to do with mining required a check voucher and a check to transfer the funds to the

LATE 1980S
One premier, as a keynote speaker at a Government Agents conference, describes Government Agent offices as "the place where the rubber hits the road."

Ministry of Mines. Needless to say, I needed help. Luckily, it was only a phone call away to my parent office in Nanaimo where Allen Watson, the mining pro, helped me step by step through the process.

"I must also mention that the free-miner also helped me during the initial stages by telling me what Taron used to do. He showed me such things as how to ensure the map sketches matched the information on the claim recorded documents.

"All in all, it ended up being an exciting experience when I began my training in the procedures for recording mining claims."

PRESENTED WITH A GOLD SCALE

Many staff have found deep family ties rooted in the history of Government Agents. Regional Director of Interior Northeast Deborah Lipscombe describes her family connections:

"As the Executive Sponsor of the Government Agent's 150 project, I have had the opportunity to express an incredible sense of pride for the organization that I work for and the people that I work with. Relatively new to Government Agents, I became the Regional Manager for the Interior/Northeast, Government Agent for Quesnel and Gold Commissioner for the Cariboo Mining Division in early 2001. From day one, I have had nothing but respect for the work that Service BC's Government Agent staff carry out every day on behalf of the citizens of British Columbia. What I did not expect was to uncover the connection that I have to the history we are celebrating.

"After taking up my initial appointment in the Cariboo and subsequent appointment for the Kamloops, Nicola, Osoyoos, Revelstoke, Similkameen and Vernon Mining Divisions, we lost my dad's cousin, John Ross, in a motorcycle accident in California. Shortly thereafter at a family wedding, my father was presented with a gold scale that belonged to his great-great grandfather, at the bequest of his late cousin. David John Evans, my great-great-great grandfather, immigrated to Canada from Wales and was both a coal miner in Nanaimo and gold miner in Barkerville, married and had five daughters and one son, leaving the gold scale to his only son, Samuel. When Samuel passed away, his wife gave the gold scales to her brother-in-law, which always irked Samuel's daughter, Mary-Beth. When the opportunity presented itself, Mary-Beth traded her crystal collection to get the gold scale back for her son, John Ross. Dad then passed the scales along to me, feeling that a home with me was most appropriate, given my role as Gold Commissioner."

A Meaningful Connection

Service BC Centre staff face the public all day long. But it can also provide the opportunity for meaningful connections with strangers. Staff in Vernon tell of one such encounter:

"Last year a very quiet, soft-spoken man came to my counter to do a simple driver's licence renewal. When I pulled up his record, I advised him of an outstanding fine he would need to pay before he could renew. He explained that he had filed for bankruptcy and this was taken care of, so I called collections for an authorization number to proceed.

"While I was on hold, I looked up at this man, and he had tears streaming down his face. He didn't make a sound; he was stone-faced. When he finally spoke, he explained that this outstanding ticket had been issued to him when he was speeding to the hospital one year ago almost to the day when his daughter was killed in a car accident. I have four kids of my own, and I couldn't help feeling this man's horrendous pain.

"I did my best to hold back my own tears and finished his renewal. However, when it came time to take his picture, I had to walk away and take a moment.

"As customer service representatives on the front counter we have the occasional ranting and raving customer and fiascos that we have to deal with. This experience taught me to put things into perspective and see what is important in life. It's the people in our lives that are important."

Late 1990s
Some Government Agent offices co-located with the federal government.

Acknowledgements

Contributions from Government Agents and their staff across British Columbia have helped shape this book and tell the story of the branch's 150 years of outstanding service to the public. The BC150 Project Team played a huge part in it as well. For a year and a half, team members worked to bring the dream of a commemorative book about the province's Government Agents to fruition.

Every attempt has been made to accredit the many people who submitted anecdotes, historical and background information, photographs, artwork, or poetry, but there may be some whose names have been unintentionally omitted. The publisher apologizes for any such errors and asks to be contacted at 250 356-2038 for corrections to future editions.

Among the various contributors, however, one person merits special recognition: Gordon Swan, Government Agent in Merritt and Princeton, spent more than a year soliciting and collecting the great number of submissions necessary for a project of this nature, and he wrote much of the material contained in this publication. To him many thanks are owed.

A special thank you to editor Patricia Freeman, whose writing and editing brought cohesion and life to the history and stories of the Government Agents.

Grateful appreciation also goes to the many individuals who shared in the making of this book:

DENIS ANHOLT, Friends of the Government: An Administrative History of British Columbia Government Agents, Victoria: University of Victoria, doctoral thesis, 1991

GEORGE BROOMFIELD, Retired Government Agent

JOYCE BROWN, Government Agent, Trail, B.C.

DANNA BURGESS, Customer Service Representative, Fernie, B.C.

DONNA CADIEUX, Past Deputy Government Agent, Nanaimo, B.C.

WENDY CLEMENT, Senior Customer Service Representative, Ashcroft, B.C.

SHEILA COPE, Senior Customer Service Representative, Invermere, B.C.

SUSAN DAHLO, North Vancouver, B.C.,
    Boundary Historical Society Report

DARLENE DRIEDIGER, Government Agent, Nakusp, B.C.

JIM EDGAR, Government Agent, Sechelt, B.C.

WAYNE HAKANSON, Government Agent, Penticton, B.C.

JAMES HAY, Government Agent, Chilliwack, B.C.

CHERYLL HEROUX, Government Agent, Maple Ridge, B.C.

CRAIG HOOPER, Poet, Vanderhoof, B.C.

AUDREY HOY, Customer Service Representative,
    Prince Rupert, B.C.

BETTE-JO HUGHES, Executive Director,
    B.C. Ministry of Labour and Citizens' Services

CARLA HUNT, Customer Service Representative, Vernon, B.C.

ED JOHANSSON, Customer Service Representative, Nanaimo, B.C.

TAMARA JOHNSON, Customer Service Representative,
    Revelstoke, B.C.

BYRON JOHNSTON, Government Agent, Duncan, B.C.

MONICA JONES, Government Agent,
    Queen Charlotte Islands/Haida Gwaii, B.C.

JULIE KELLY, Government Agent, Nanaimo, B.C.

PETER LEE, Regional Director, Nelson, B.C.

DEBORAH LIPSCOMBE, Regional Director, Kamloops, B.C.

JEFF MacKENZIE, Government Agent, Campbell River, B.C.

CONNIE MADSEN, Customer Service Representative,
    Cranbrook, B.C.

DAN MARTIN, Retired Government Agent, Grand Forks, B.C.

DIANA McDONALD, Customer Service Representative,
    Invermere, B.C.

CATHY O'CONNOR, Customer Service Representative, Vernon, B.C.

JEAN PATTERSON, local historian, Burns Lake, B.C.

2007
The new Prince George Service BC Centre opens its doors, marking the first of many new welcoming offices open to the public and creating a more welcoming face to government in communities.

Robin Potts, Government Agent, Courtenay, B.C.

Wendy Robinson, Project Director,
    B.C. Ministry of Labour and Citizens' Services

Peter Rodseth, Artist, Vanderhoof, B.C.

Susan Salter, Customer Service Representative, Smithers, B.C.

Susan Schienbein, Government Agent, Vanderhoof, B.C.

Debbie Schroeter, Government Agent,
    Cranbrook, Fernie, and Sparwood, B.C.

Jennifer Smyth, Director of Corporate Communications and
    Change Management, B.C. Ministry of Labour and Citizens' Services

James Spalding, Government Agent, Port Alberni, B.C.

Lynne Stonier-Newman, author and historian,
    Little Heffley Lake, B.C.

Lawrie Sutton, Customer Service Representative,
    Maple Ridge, B.C.

Amber Swan, Student, Thompson Rivers University,
    Kamloops, B.C.

Gordon Swan, Government Agent, Merritt, B.C.

Geraldine Taron, Customer Service Representative,
    Nanaimo, B.C.

Mark Timmins, Service BC Project Manager,
    B.C. Ministry of Employment and Income Assistance, Kamloops, B.C.

James Torrance, Retired Government Agent, Penticton, B.C.

Melody Wey, Internal Communications Co-ordinator,
    B.C. Ministry of Labour and Citizens' Services

Lisa Wilsgard, Customer Service Representative,
    Golden, B.C.

Lorne Wilson, Government Agent, Squamish, B.C.

Robert Woods, Government Agent, Powell River, B.C.

Today

The public can get access to government information and services in person at Service BC Centres in 59 locations across the province, by phone, in person or online. Service BC: access to government services made easy.

Photo Credits

P. 2   (Government Agents Day proclamation)
        courtesy of Ministry of Attorney General;

p. 10   (St. Andrew's Hospital) courtesy of Royal BC Museum, BC Archives;

p. 11   (weather report of 1902 and weather report of 1908)
        courtesy of Princeton Museum and Archives;

p. 12   (Fort Street, Victoria) courtesy of Royal BC Museum, BC Archives;

p. 14   (November 1926 letter) courtesy of Gordon Swan, Government Agent,
        Merritt, B.C.;

p. 15   (January 1939 letter) courtesy of Gordon Swan, Government Agent,
        Merritt, B.C.;

p. 16   (May 1942 letter) courtesy of Gordon Swan, Government Agent,
        Merritt, B.C.;

p. 17   (March 1870 letter) courtesy of Royal BC Museum, BC Archives;

p. 19   (Greenwood Courthouse and Police Headquarters)
        courtesy of Royal BC Museum, BC Archives;

p. 25   (Clinton's local dignitaries) courtesy of Royal BC Museum, BC Archives;

p. 26   (Pouce Coupe, B.C.) courtesy of Royal BC Museum, BC Archives;

p. 27   (colonial officials) courtesy of Royal BC Museum, BC Archives;

p. 29   (Thomas Elwyn) courtesy of Royal BC Museum, BC Archives;

p. 41   (Lytton Stage) courtesy of Royal BC Museum, BC Archives;

p. 42   (Fence Line, Cariboo) courtesy of Royal BC Museum, BC Archives;

p. 49   (Walter Scott) courtesy of Nakusp Museum and Archives;

p. 51   (bones of Aeneas Dewar) courtesy of Jason Wood,
        British Columbia History - Vol. 38 No.1 2005;

p. 51   (Aeneas Dewar) courtesy of Vernon Museum and Archives;

p. 52   (Fred Soues) courtesy of Terry Lush, Sr. Customer Service Representative,
        Clinton, B.C.;